RESTORING
RELATIONSHIPS

RESTORING RELATIONSHIPS

5 THINGS TO TRY BEFORE YOU SAY GOODBYE

PETER M. KALELLIS

A Crossroad Book
The Crossroad Publishing Company
New York

The Crossroad Publishing Company
481 Eighth Avenue, New York, NY 10001

Printed in the United States of America

Library of Congress Cataloging-in-Publication Data

Kalellis, Peter M.
    Restoring relationships : five things to try before you say goodbye /
  Peter Kalellis.
      p. cm.
    Includes bibliographical references.
    ISBN 0-8245-1880-2 (alk. paper)
    1. Man-woman relationships. 2. Interpersonal communication.
    3. Interpersonal relations. 4. Marriage. I. Title.
    HQ801 .K28 2000
    306.7–dc21
                                        00-011133

2   3   4   5   6   7   8   9   10   06   05   04   03   02   01

CONTENTS

Four
COMMUNICATE AND CONNECT

Five
LOVE AND LIVE LONGER

ACKNOWLEDGMENTS

With genuine gratitude, I would like to thank the following individuals for their untiring support and cooperation in making this
book a reality:

Reid Boates, a literary agent, who gave me the name and the
idea for the book and who encouraged me to complete it.

My dear friend Ernie Anastos, TV news anchor, who read my
first draft and presented important issues for me to consider as I
developed my theme.

Margery Hueston, who worked diligently on the first draft.

Patti Lawrence, friend and coeditor, whose insights far exceeded
the words in each chapter.

John Eagleson, who worked on my previous book, *Pick Up
Your Couch and Walk,* and who made sure that my thoughts came
across effectively.

Paul McMahon, directing editor, and John Tintera, marketing
manager, at Crossroad Publishing Company, whose visions for
this book reflect my own drive to help couples strengthen their
relationships.

My clients over the years, with whom I have shared sensitive
therapeutic relationships. Although some of their stories are incor-
porated here, their names were changed to protect their privacy.

My wife, Pat, whose encouragement, ideas, comments, and
loving support keep refueling my energy and inspiration.

My children, Katina, Basil, Michael, and Mercene, whose joy
about my writing keeps me going even when my own enthusiasm
falters.

A last and very special word of appreciation goes to Gwendolin
Herder, CEO/publisher of Crossroad Publishing Company, who
upon hearing the title and proposal of my book showed immediate
interest.

PROLOGUE

Tom and Tracy sit across from me; simulated smiles disguise their nervousness. They shift positions in their chairs and seem resentful and impatient. Their turbulent seven-year-old marriage is now on the rocks. A lawyer friend sent them to me as a last resort before they took their case to the divorce court.

Tracy is thirty-four, but her frustration, hostility, and rage make her seem older. Tom, thirty-eight, in a sullen mask of "nothing-is-wrong," cannot understand why they are here. It is hard to believe that seven years ago this couple was very much in love and confident that life without each other would be meaningless.

During the first session, I learn that they have two children, a four-year-old boy and a fourteen-month-old girl. In kindergarten the four-year-old acts out, biting and hitting other children. The little girl wakes up several times every night and cries. They are victims of a damaged relationship. Already in an insecure and un-stable environment, an acrimonious divorce will scar the children for life.

Not with words but with their expressions, the parents plead: Can this therapist do something for us? Can he bring peace, love, and joy back into our marriage?

I react in my own way: I'm not a miracle worker, but I'll try to help you rebuild your marriage. I'll provide guidelines if you will apply them with honesty and patient persistence.

This book is an invitation to explore *Five Things to Try before You Say Goodbye.*

INTRODUCTION

This book is intended not to impress, but to encourage readers and their partners to reinvent their potential and reconsider their relationships before abandoning them. The human relationship is the most personal, the deepest, and potentially the most beautiful experience two human beings can share. But it can also be a complex, most troublesome and painful experience when two people feel dissatisfied with their individual selves and with the way they relate to each other. Unresolved issues of their past — some originating with their individual families or their cultural-political backgrounds — unmet needs of the present, or harbored hells and furies could cause a gradual deterioration and eventual death to their relationship.

The vision that substantiates this book grew out of the long-term experience of many married and unmarried couples whose troubled lives sent them to therapy. Some of their stories may be considered cautionary tales that might be useful to the reader; others may be disturbing. In all, they indicate our human predicament.

The five parts of this book summarize choices that made the difference to the couples' relationships and nurtured positive approaches to their lives together. Not all couples reported success in implementing all the suggestions in this book; perhaps they were not ready for full implementation. Some couples needed to apply all five parts with equal effort and intensity while others used the sections that applied specifically to their situation. Essentially, though, each part proved to be of vital importance to those who sincerely sought reconciliation and who wanted to improve their relationship.

Assuming that you feel responsible for the quality of your relationship with your spouse, friend, or lover, the five areas to consider are:

1. *Surrender, Make a New Beginning:*
   Without reservations, make a personal commitment to work creatively and honestly. In this part of the book you will find ideas, directives, and suggestions to encourage and strengthen your effort. As you work with patience and persistence to pursue your goal of reconciliation, you need to consider and remove the obstacles you may encounter along the way.

2. *Dispense Your Anger Wisely:*
   Anger is a major obstacle to human interaction, especially within significant relationships. It is an emotion that needs to be dealt with and dissipated effectively in order to avoid its catastrophic consequences. You will be amazed as you learn about the origins of anger and how they affect both body and soul. You need to know how to understand this emotion, not as an enemy but as a friend.

3. *Forgive and Feel Free:*
   Reading this part of the book may prove to be a liberating experience for you. You will learn that you don't need to have divine qualities to forgive the person who has betrayed you, wronged you, or done you an injustice. The four chapters in this section will help you find the inner strength needed to enable you to let go of the hurts that hinder your life. Ideally, as your damaged emotions heal, your relationship will improve immensely. With a sense of restored self-image, you will enjoy clarity of mind and a new ability to connect with your partner.

4. *Communicate and Connect:*
   The opposite of communication is emotional death. This part of the book transcends analytical theories about defective dialogues and gives a practical overview of how two people can talk in an honest, symmetrical, and loving way, and can share a heart-to-heart dialogue that promises a deepened relationship with increased intimacy.

5. *Love and Live Longer:*
   Smile! What happiness it is to love! Love is a strong emotion that can bring the greatest joy to human life. It brings about life itself. Beyond romantic illusions, naive myths, or theo-

retical abstractions, this part of your reading explores what love really is and what it takes to cultivate the ability to be a loving and lovable person.

To get the most from this book, consider reading it slowly, underlining the parts that appeal to you, summarizing other parts and reading the summaries again at a later time. Write down some of your thoughts. Embrace the idea that you are fully in charge of your personal life and that you are capable of improving its quality. Above all, equip yourself with feelings of hope and courage. Anything is possible if you are willing to do the work. And when you have tried, you will know the deep satisfaction of a sincere effort to bring reconciliation and love to your relationship.

~ ONE ~

SURRENDER, MAKE A NEW BEGINNING

*If you truly want your relationship
to work and improve,
surrender yourself to that goal
for as long as it takes to achieve it.*

❧

*The possibility of being hurt again
is far less dangerous to you in the long run
than loneliness.*

Chapter 1

YES OR NO?

When we pollute our relationships with unloving thoughts, or destroy or abort them with unloving attitudes, we are threatening our emotional survival.
— MARIANNE WILLIAMSON

You are holding this book for a reason. You may be hurting or confused over a marriage or a relationship that has been disturbing you for a long time. You may even feel threatened with what is ahead: a break in communications, a separation, or even a divorce. You are doing everything possible to avoid confrontation with your partner, and sometimes you are able to create the most ingenious plans to prevent pain or to put a Band-Aid on the bleeding wound, loneliness.

Do you want your relationship to improve and to last? If your answer is "No, I've had it; I've tried everything and nothing works," then this book is not for you. You have made up your mind that your relationship is irreparable. It is over.

But suppose that in the privacy of your mind there is a ray of hope that touches your heart and evokes lingering feelings of love and compassion. Although you hesitate to admit it, you want to say, "Yes, I want this marriage to work; this relationship is important to me. I want to restore it." If this is the case, then this book is written for you. Stay with it.

As soon as you say yes to yourself, shift your thoughts and emotional center toward loving and working with patience toward yes and away from no. Simply, surrender yourself to your goal and give yourself time, as long as it takes — three months, six months, nine months — to have purposeful encounters with your partner. The word "surrender" may appear scary to you, but sometimes

17

what seems like surrender isn't that at all. It's about what's going on in your hearts. It's about seeing clearly the way life is, accepting it, and being true to it, whatever the pain, because the pain of not being true to it is far, far greater. Make reconciliation the first priority in your life.

During this period, things will not be easy, let alone immediately productive. Certain well-intentioned rescuers may try to persuade you that reconciling with your partner is a pipe dream. "It never works," they'll say. "Get yourself another partner who can love you and make you happy." With or without these "rescuers," doubts about the future success of this relationship will resurface in your mind. This is normal, for in spite of earnest efforts to make the relationship work, sometimes you will err and clash; fragile feelings will get hurt. We are not perfect. You simply must trust that patience and persistence can perform miracles.

Give yourself permission to make a new beginning.

⋘⋙

You are sensitive, scared, afraid; you do not want to get hurt again. You must fight the urge to withdraw, to recoil. Fight it with the very powerful idea that very often the negative thought you may have about your partner is something you are thinking about yourself.

When Peggy, a lawyer in a prestigious firm, learned that her husband had an affair, she did not display any angry reaction, but deep in her heart she felt hurt and betrayed. Bernie had committed adultery. Since the night he had confessed his mistake, their love life, previously intimate and happy, was blighted. "It was just a fling," she rationalized, "a common event in our times. I can rise above my anger. It can happen to anyone. I almost had an affair myself — with a colleague — but I was able to control my impulses." However, the reality of what he had done nagged her painfully. "How can I trust him again?"

Bernie, a brilliant civil engineer in his mid-forties, had been married to Peggy for twenty years. Their only daughter was a junior in college. "There's a lot of love in my relationship with Peg," he claimed, "but six months ago I blew it." He was angry with himself. "How did I succumb to such stupidity? It meant nothing to me."

People today often seem eager to confess to this type of lapse, and they confess it to the very person it hurts most. Six months after his brief affair, guilt-ridden Bernie told Peggy of his fall from grace when he was in Japan on business for his company. Remorsefully, he told his wife how sorry he was. He believed she forgave him, and he felt much better for being such an honest man.

Bernie's confession was not a mature and loving act. *Honesty expressed for the wrong intention is the worst form of hostility.* Did Bernie know that? He wanted to relieve himself from the burden of his guilt — truly a wrong intention. Furthermore, perhaps unconsciously, he wanted to test his wife: Will she continue to love me as much even when I reveal something ugly about myself?

Mature love would have prompted him to say, "I messed up. It was my wrongdoing, my cross to bear. I have no right to free myself of my guilt at my partner's expense. I can seek help and counsel from a minister, priest, rabbi, therapist, close friend. They can provide me with some relief.

Although there was enough love in Peggy's heart to forgive Bernie, the scar remained raw and sensitive for a long time. However, with the help of a therapist, she took a personal inventory to explore areas that needed improvement for herself and for the marriage. She focused on the positive qualities of their relationship. In spite of his violation of his marital vows, Bernie was a thoughtful, sensitive, hard working, good man with whom she had shared wonderful years together. "We took delightful vacations, traveled oversees, played and prayed together, and built a beautiful home for ourselves. If I can let go of the hurt he has caused me and be a better mate to him, he will be capable of being a better mate to me. In my heart I know he can. We can still have a productive life together." As she pondered these thoughts, Peggy felt an inner strength.

When she shared her thoughts with Bernie, he agreed that their emotional investment was too precious to let go. "We must work together to maintain and develop what we have, each other," he said gratefully. "I promise to do my best to be a good husband." Ultimately, their efforts to be attentive to each other's needs resulted in making their relationship stronger.

Sometimes we think and feel that so much is wrong that we come to accept defeat. "There is nothing I can do," we may say.

But every negative thought and its precipitating feeling are potential energy toward a better way of being. Give yourself time and space to move toward what could be right and beneficial for you. Replace negative thoughts (the wrongs that your partner has done) with positive ones (the good qualities that your partner is capable of contributing to your relationship), and you will feel better and stronger. Avoid the notion that you must be right all the time; just do what seems right to you. It is a difficult art, and it calls for awareness, skill, and patience. But it can be learned; and those who learn it have in their hands the means of restoring a positive relationship as partners without violating the integrity of each other's identity.

The Strength within You

What if, instead of vacillating, you were to make a commitment to work hard, giving your relationship a new chance? What if you were to believe that within you lies the power to bring about a change in your life? Get deeper into yourself and learn from your inner self what you must do, advises an ancient Greek adage. And Elisabeth Kübler-Ross adds, "Learn to be in touch with the silence within yourself and know that everything in this life has a purpose." Think about it: these are things that you decide on your own, by yourself, for yourself.

Your physical body is at work every moment. Your heart beats, your lungs breathe, your eyes see, your ears hear, your hair grows; you don't have to make them work — they just do. When we suffer some physical damage, a physician treats the ailing part with medication, but healing takes place on its own. The broken bone mends, the injured part heals as long as we don't do anything to prevent the healing process.

Your spiritual self, your soul, yearns for reconciliation and peace. In addition to the physical, material, and legal aspects of your marriage or relationship there is an emotional involvement as well. It needs special attention. Like your physical growth and survival, your relationship needs ongoing care and responsibility. All of your best qualities — and none more so than your own *natural* yearning for reconciliation — need to be activated and put in motion for the restoration and safekeeping of your relationship.

The Johnsons, a young couple in their early thirties and married for seven years, had a turbulent relationship. Marriage did not meet their expectations. Eventually they agreed that they did not care enough for each other to maintain the marriage much longer. And since both came from broken homes, divorce appeared to be a viable solution. Each one engaged an attorney, and by the time they appeared in court, they had incurred over twelve thousand dollars of debt in legal fees. In a preliminary hearing, the judge instructed the Johnsons to seek the help of a marriage therapist for at least six weeks before returning to the court. It was at this point that they came to me to discuss their situation.

Both were scarred emotionally and mired in anger. It was some time before they mentioned they had three children. In a tearful angry scene, the wife removed her wedding ring and flung it at her husband as a symbolic and official gesture that the marriage was over. She informed me that four weeks after witnessing the birth of their third child, her husband had left her and had moved in with an old friend, where he lived the life of a bachelor.

The couple looked at each other with contempt. They did not appear to have any intention of reconciling.

"What are you looking for?" I asked.

After a prolonged silence, the wife said, "He left me and our three children, and now he lives with his friends. He doesn't take any responsibility as a father or husband."

"I send you money, don't I?"

"Keep your money. The children need their father."

"I left because I never felt appreciated."

"That's nonsense. I'm a mother of three and I work. What else do you want from me?"

"Sex," he shouted in anger.

The debate became so inflammatory, so verbally abusive that I had to interrupt them. "This not a boxing ring. There is no sense in throwing punches at each other," I said.

"We fight like this all the time," she said.

"We've made up our minds. Divorce is the solution." He sounded determined.

"You have made up your mind. I don't want a divorce," she said.

"Let me help you with your decision," I offered.

"I guess it's over." She looked as if her spirit were broken.

"It was a mistake; we don't belong together," he added.

"If you had no children," I said, "divorce would not be so difficult. But, tell me, how are you going to look into the eyes of your children and tell them that you are mutilating the family, that you are changing the structure of their world by a process of radical surgery that will make all their tomorrows different. I have to tell you, the way you treat each other lacks responsibility."

I could see Mr. Johnson's face turn red with anger. The word "responsibility" touched a sensitive chord. His wife's eyes widened in wonder.

"I'll give her whatever she wants. I want out."

"I want you to come back."

"I don't love you anymore."

"You don't know how I feel."

"I don't care."

"What about the children?" She wept.

The natural inclination of all parents is to spare their children from as much pain as humanly possible. When the Johnsons told their children of the impending divorce, the two older ones cried inconsolably. Their eyes were ringed with dark circles, and acute grief of human hurt showed on their pale faces. They kept asking, "Why, Mommy?"

"Why, Dad? Can't you do something to fix it?"

As the Johnsons reported the reaction of their children, I studied their profiles and felt somewhat prophetic. They felt shaken and anxious about the condition of their children. This marriage could be salvaged, I thought, if I could convey to these two that what they really need is respect for each other and responsibility for what they created together, their family.

When they came back for their sixth session, complying with the court's mandate, they asked me if they could continue their marital therapy for a few more sessions.

"That's what I'm here for," I said with a smile. As I marked their next appointment in my book, Richard Taylor's statement surfaced in my mind: There are many things holding married people together besides love, and these are sometimes sufficient even when there is little or no love in the marriage.

In one of the sessions, I asked the Johnsons to describe what their marriage was like after the arrival of their third child. They agreed that child bearing and caring did not leave much room for intimacy and romance. As the responsibilities of married life increased, they pulled away from each other emotionally. Physically, they shared the same bed, ate at the same dinner table, watched the same TV, talked but didn't really communicate, and halfheartedly parented their children. Occasionally they had sex, but they didn't feel love. Gradually, they moved into a state of cold isolation and experienced feelings of anger and loneliness.

In marital therapy, the Johnsons gradually matured to recognize the potential in themselves and in their marriage. They recognized how important it was to share feelings and thoughts as responsible mates to avoid emotional isolation, a destructive force. Step by step, they learned to discuss small disagreements before they became major conflicts and allowed each other to have their own opinions. Almost in every session, the emotional state of the children became a focal point. Increasingly, they became aware of how their dysfunctional interaction had affected the children and decided to become creatively involved with them. Meanwhile, they spent special time together every Friday night, telling each other of their love and celebrating. Today, five years later, they are still together.

Far from being dead and done for, your relationship can be resurrected and revived. The person that you are at this point needs and deserves a new kind of relationship, one without negativity, hostility, and all the bad perceptions that have caused alienation and pain. A new relationship is exactly what you will see emerging from the ashes as you try to be sensitive to your mate's needs. While other marriages are dying, yours can spring into a new life, because you have said yes.

When Mind and Heart Cooperate

Our contemporary culture has become most sophisticated in the avoidance of pain, not only physical pain, but also emotional and mental discomfort. We live a life of denial, preferring anesthesia to the pursuit of a solution. We panic or become defensive when a sudden misunderstanding leaves us off balance. Our relationship struggles on while we use our very fallible minds, our thoughts, as anesthesia to mask the very pain whose purpose it is to pinpoint our problems.

Instead of using our fallible thoughts to become bitter, what if we were to yield to the wisdom of our hearts and pursue a more creative response? When the answer to our problem remains hanging between our minds and our hands, it remains weak and superficial. If we simply react to a situation, then our frustration becomes self-righteous, our hope for improvement degenerates into a desire for quick results, and our patience is soon exhausted by disappointment. Only when our mind has descended into our heart can we expect a lasting response and potential resolution to well up from our innermost self.

In your search for resolution and reconciliation, the visible changes that take place will not be as noticeable as you want or expect. Temporarily you may struggle with doubts: Is it ever going to work? Remind yourself that these doubts come from the mind, which demands results, not from the heart, which yearns on an organic level for reconciliation. If things seem hopeless, then listen to Antoine de Saint-Exupéry's voice from *The Little Prince:* "It is only with the heart that one can see rightly; what is essential is invisible to the eye."

What is essential is invisible to the eye. What do these words mean to you in your personal effort to reconcile? Could they mean that each of you may experience different feelings in the same situation? How would you know unless you try?

Ask your heart: How willing am I to trust my real self to my partner? What will it take? Do I feel worthwhile? Should I risk the effort of reentering a relationship without a guarantee? Could I endure the feeling of not immediately knowing the results of my efforts?

What makes this process difficult for each of us is that we have developed a fundamental orientation toward interpersonal relations, thoughts, feelings, and behaviors to expect in the present what we have experienced in the past. It takes renewed courage and work to challenge these biases and risk reentry into our relationship. When mind and heart work together, the change is already in motion, converting anxiety into compassion. A compassionate person can no longer look at the destructive qualities of the other without seeing them as an opportunity for self-restoration and restoration of the other.

I invite you to take time out and think. Do you want to restore this relationship? Then stay put, relax, be quiet for a few minutes, and listen attentively to your own struggle. I know it is difficult to take these initial steps. You may doubt your own abilities, your own strength. You may wish to find someone, some charismatic professional to solve your problem. However, when you cease listening to external voices and allow your soul to speak, you may come to sense that in the midst of your sadness there is joy, in the midst of your confusion there is direction, in the midst of your fear there is peace, in the midst of your helplessness there is strength. It is your strength that needs to be applied once you have said yes.

You are not a puppet on a string waiting for someone to pull and push you into a performance. I cannot push you into anything. Nobody has that right. You are in charge of your life, as you ought to be. You can make things happen; you can create the difference — not in a selfish or capricious manner to serve your personal interests, but in an intentional way to seek reconciliation. A miracle? Yes, a miracle that you will make possible for yourself.

Are you still in doubt? Then try to repeat, at least three times a day, a statement by the incomparable Martha Graham: "There is a vitality, a life force, an energy, a quickening that is translated through you into action, and because there is only one of you in all time, this expression is unique. And if you block it, it will never exist through any other medium and will be lost."

If you believe that within you there is a vitality, an energy that can be translated into action, it is time to stand tall and seek healing. Make the first move. Be the first to start the restoration process.

"But that's not fair!" you protest.

Fair or not, one person has to care enough about the relationship to take that first step — maybe even by going all the way to meet the other partner. Since you are the one reading this book, the responsibility falls on your shoulders. Of course, total success will come when both partners work at restoration. If you do diligently what is required of you, and your partner remains totally unresponsive, the relationship will suffer; however, you yourself will have peace, knowing that you have done everything possible to restore the relationship.

Ponder the following suggestions one at a time and try to consider a good way to apply each one. If one is not working, have faith that there is more to learn. As you think about these suggestions and apply them, your skills will improve, and you will realize what else is needed. Focus on the process, not the outcome. Growth takes place in spurts. If you concentrate on the degree of success of each idea, you will become anxious. You cannot insist that your efforts have predictable outcomes. Remind yourself that you are on a journey during which you hope to restore your relationship. Don't be in a hurry to arrive at your destination. You are in a state of restoration, you have a feeling that you could have a better relationship, which is your ultimate goal. Straighten your shoulders, walk more resolutely, face and talk to your partner with energy and verve. Feel those emotions that lead to harmony. Most of all, try to cherish the process; do not hurry the journey at all.

For Your Consideration

~ Learn the language of love. Saying yes implies that you are willing to give your relationship a new chance. A new chance implies a different approach to relating with your partner to attain positive results. You may need to start speaking gently; you are speaking to a human being, not to an object. You need a different language, the language of love.

~ Be lovable. Our deepest human need is to be loved, to be engaged. It is a wonderful feeling when someone truly loves you. You still need to be loved by your partner even though you have been deeply hurt in the relationship. Naturally, you are afraid that you may be rejected and hurt again. It can happen. But the possibility of being hurt again is far less dangerous to you in the long run than loneliness.

~ Give the gift of love. In a new beginning, if you come into the relationship as a lovable person, it is unlikely that you will be rejected. You are sensitive; your partner is sensitive. Looking at each other with hostility or suspicion, or harboring an ulterior motive can make you both very fragile. Bring new life into the relationship by offering the gift of love, not just to your partner, not just to yourself, but to the relationship.

~ Monitor your demands. If you expect your partner to fulfill all your needs, you are asking for more than any single human being can provide. You will have greater success if you nurture the emerging needs of your relationship.

~ Be caring and loving. Approach your partner with a sense of gentle openness, welcoming the opportunity to make this contact with caring and loving feelings. Focus on your goal as you release everything that you have been told is impossible or unrealistic, and allow yourself the freedom to make your new contact with your partner possible for you.

~ Make haste slowly. Do not be too eager to express all your emotions and ideas at your first encounter. Become interested in the response of your partner and appreciate what the present makes available to you.

~ Remove assumptions. Assumptions are obstacles created by the mind. For example: Other people have better relationships than I do. Many human interactions are free from problems. A conflict in a relationship is abnormal and destructive, and therefore it should be avoided. Good relationships go more smoothly. Why are *they* so happy and *we* are so tense and miserable?

~ Beware of the control concept. No one wants to be controlled by another. Mind-driven statements such as, "I know how much we can spend!" and, "I know I'm right on this," are much more stressful than heart-driven comments such as, "Let's figure this out together."

~ Try not to change your partner. People change if they realize that a change is necessary, not because you tell them to change. Part of change can be to discover, even slowly, the joy of sharing a life together.

Chapter 2

THE NEW ATTEMPT

*Being human always means reaching out beyond oneself —
reaching out for something other than oneself — for something or someone, for a meaning to fulfill, or for another
human being to love.* — VICTOR E. FRANKL

A marriage or a relationship can work only favorably if both
partners are willing to cooperate, to work together to fulfill
each other's needs, and to create a climate in which both can
grow, mature, and share life. It cannot be done by one person
alone; it cannot be forced upon anyone. The person who becomes
aware that something is wrong in the relationship must initiate
an attempt to repair it — not tonight or tomorrow, but steadily,
over time.

Put differently, because you have said yes, you must commit
yourself to the process of change. This is a process that starts with
yourself and then moves through the relationship. Do you often
feel that conflict has become the norm, as if some sinister force
from outside has invaded your relationship and taken charge of
your life, threatening to destroy your love? The usual reaction to
conflict is panic followed by flight or, in a relationship, an effort
to evade and suppress it.

What if, instead of avoidance, we take another look at conflict
itself? What happens if we view conflict as an integral part of a
healthy relationship? What if conflict provides essential information that partners need for personal growth and for the maturity of
their relationship? What if conflict, far from being a deadly enemy,
is in fact a friend in disguise?

Differences are unavoidable. They are what make you unique.
You have lived separate lives for perhaps twenty years or more,

during which time each of you has developed a set of individual tastes, preferences, habits, likes and dislikes, values and standards. It is totally unreasonable to suppose that two people, just because they love each other, should always want to do the same thing in the same way at the same time.

Think for a moment how different you are from your partner. Besides the biological differences, you may be of different cultural, ethnic, educational, and religious backgrounds. Your upbringings may be different. Differences influence your style of life, but they can also enrich your life. Similarities initially tend to be the magnet that attracts us to each other. We like the same things, we have the same ambitions, the same tastes, the same friends, the same hopes and dreams. Great! For some people, similarities seem sufficient to hold them together for a lifetime. There's nothing wrong with that. For others, as they grow and their needs change, similarities no longer give them the same satisfaction. They begin to compare and compete — anything you can do, I can do better — and they engage in a power struggle. Trouble begins.

Tennis, which Bob and Jean enjoyed every weekend, became a contest in which each was determined to be the winner. Bob, who also played racquetball with his friends, excelled in tennis, and he usually won. "I wish he'd let me win a few games," Jean thought. It reached the stage where she no longer wanted to play with him. Her disappointment inevitably surfaced in other areas.

Mark and Cathy were carbon copies of each other as far as likes and dislikes were concerned. They were animal lovers, and each owned a cat. When they joined their lives, they were delighted to have their cats in their new home and treated them as if they were their children. When their strong romantic feelings subsided, the joy in caring for their cats also faded. Cleaning, brushing, and taking them to the veterinarian became major tasks that both resisted. Who was to be responsible for these jobs became an issue. Arguments and anger arose, causing silence and distance between the two.

For many couples, difference in religion often becomes a point of contention. As long as there is smooth sailing, religion is respected. When disagreements become conflicts, however, some people point a blaming finger and say, "This would not have happened to us if we had been of the same faith." The other partner becomes defensive and trouble begins.

Differences — and we are all different from each other — can be a significant contribution to relationship, provided that each person honors and respects the background of the other. Partners who are proud of their cultural background may introduce it into their relationship as a positive factor which may enhance their relationship. However, it needs to be introduced with sensitivity, not with a spirit of superiority. "My culture is better than yours," or "My religion is the true religion," will not work. Introducing cultural differences into a relationship needs to be done with good intentions and a desire to enrich the life of the other, not to control it.

Like most therapists I have found that similarities and differences do not cause conflicts, rifts, and eventually divorce or separation. Rather, the cause lies in the inability of the partners to see what is good in the relationship and to assume the responsibility needed to make the relationship work.

Being different is not the problem. The problem is how our differentness affects the relationship. For example, how do you express your thoughts? How do you make your needs and wishes known to your partner? Your response to these questions is of great importance. If you are a wife and you are frustrated because not only are you holding a job outside the home, but you are also carrying the entire load of duties within the home — housework, care of the children, shopping, and paying the bills on time — how do you convey your feelings to your husband who seems disinterested?

If you are a hard-working husband, "busting your tail" and determined to be a success in the world, both for personal fulfillment and for the welfare of your family, understandably you want to sit in front of the television and unwind. How do you share your needs with your spouse?

If both partners continue to confront each other in states of frustration, eventually their wills will clash, resulting in a quarrel, a fight: "How can you sit and watch that stupid game while I'm slaving trying to put a meal on the table? The kids haven't done their homework yet."

"Can't a guy get some rest after a hard day's work?"

"Fine. Watch TV. I don't care anymore. You're useless."

Accusations made in an aggressive or hostile tone serve only one purpose: they disengage the couple. Although the disagreement is recognized, the solution is put off indefinitely. The attempt to become more deeply involved with each other in a particular area of their relationship fizzles to nothing. Alienation sets in, and in this state of discomfort and doubt, the partners question the situation: "Did I make a mistake in committing my life to this person? I thought we were in love with each other."

Suppose that when your emotions heat up you visualize the conflict as a friend in disguise; instead of getting into a fight, you examine these hot emotions and try to understand your own feelings: Why am I so angry? Why is this issue so important to me? Why am I bent out of shape?

Once you understand your own contributions to the conflict, you will eventually understand your partner's reaction. It will then be possible to turn the conflict to good account by working together to resolve the original difference through an adjustment or compromise. Of course this is oversimplified. Differences between partners that cannot be easily adjusted may have to be tolerated. But if you consider the possibility that out of each conflict comes a new opportunity, you may use this opportunity to rediscover what is good in your relationship. If you truly wish to restore your relationship, the key that opens the door to reconciliation is in your hands. Return to your partner with an open mind and gracious heart, trusting your own ability and good intentions. For a precious moment, visualize a setting where the two of you are sitting across from each other, and, being relaxed, you are able to relate and communicate in an open, honest, harmonious, and loving way. You may say it can never happen. You're right. It can never happen if you are not willing to try. But suppose you entertain the concept as possible, and with a sincere desire you develop a mental image of reaching out.

As a good start, let us focus on your strengths. You are aware of who you are, a mature adult with a genuine intention. Your intention is to give the relationship another chance. Initiate a new approach by prohibiting games that are immature and childish. If you refer to yesterday's errors, you will miss the mark. I call this insidious invader J.B. NAG, an acronym for Judgment, Blame, Negativity, Anger, and Guilt. If the existence of this five-headed monster is allowed to continue, it will sap all your strength, and any new direction will seem dark and difficult. We have all made our share of mistakes. So what! Let it go! When you feel judgmental, blaming, negative, angry, and guilty about your personal life, just drive J.B. NAG away. Don't try to reason with him, because J.B. NAG is unreasonable and destructive. Take full responsibility for all the events of your life and blame no one else. Release the idea from your mind that a failing relationship makes you a failure. Remind yourself that every negative thought you have about another person may be a projection of your own mind. It is something you may be thinking about yourself. You have the ability and wisdom to replace these negative thoughts with positive ones. As you manage more and more to make this substitution of positive for negative, you will notice an amazing difference in your feelings. Release everything that you have been thinking is impossible or unrealistic, and allow yourself the freedom to make a new attempt, totally utilizing your own energies. Release the notion that you can change another person. If there is a change to be made, let your partner process it and make the needed change. Suspend your need for external approval, including your partner's; practical and profound as they may be, the opinions of others are not yours. If you discover something worthwhile in them, you may adopt it. But get on with your purpose. Think of Victor Frankl's statement: "Being human always means reaching out beyond oneself — reaching out for something other than oneself — for something or someone, for a meaning to fulfill, or another human being to love."

Stage Your Happiness

Jay Haley, a renowned family therapist, speaks with confidence of his success with troubled couples. He gives them an uncommon activity: "Pretend. I want you both to go home and pretend that you are happy. For an entire week, anything that you do for each other will have to be positive. Speak gently and act as if you are happy together."

Haley claims that when the couple returns a week later, each partner looks and feels better. In a more relaxed state, the couple usually wants to continue the activity for at least another week. The good feelings that they experience encourage them to repeat the activity. As paradoxical as this pretend activity may seem, it speaks clearly about human behavior. You can honestly stage your personal happiness.

You have a choice. Don't feel discouraged if you don't immediately feel successful in your attempt to reconcile. You don't have to do your best, because your best leaves no room for improvement. You will have better success if you get started and simply enjoy this new attempt. You will be surprised how different you will feel simply because you have taken the initiative.

A fifty-one-year-old man named Tom called me one day for help for his "dysfunctional" relationship. He explained that his two sons were on their own now and that his wife, Wanda, was unwilling to work on the marriage with him; she wanted out, but he desperately wanted to improve his relationship with her. Tom came to me once a week for twelve weeks, eager to work hard for his own personal growth — mainly to chisel off some bad habits and to be a better husband. Wanda refused to cooperate, and at times Tom felt discouraged. I helped him develop a six-month plan for his marriage, one that he could work on by himself.

In the ninth week, my phone rang. "Doctor, this is Wanda. Tom is my husband and I believe he has been seeing you for therapy."

"How can I help you?" I asked.

"Months ago, Tom asked me to join him in therapy, but I didn't believe it could help. Our marriage was too far gone," she said. "But now I feel differently. He has changed in the last month. I don't know what you did to him, but he certainly has improved. I guess I also need to come and see you."

In the next session, I shook Tom's hand and congratulated him on his persistence. It took courage and patience for Tom to give everything he had in an effort to make his relationship better in spite of his wife's initial refusal to give him another chance. Wanda was in therapy for seven weeks when Tom began to see his once foundering marriage come back to life. It took a dedicated spouse to make the difference.

It was interesting to observe Tom at the time of his rejection by his wife; he felt lonely and discouraged. As he spoke about his frustration, he became aware of his contribution to the marriage, and he began to develop a feeling of compassion. As a compassionate man he could no longer focus on Wanda's disturbing defects; rather, he was able to see them as an opportunity to respond more tenderly to her needs and become a better husband. In the process, he rediscovered some good qualities in his wife. He not only praised her, he also rewarded her good qualities by a present, or a dinner date, or an offer to do some chores around the house. His efforts evoked positive feelings in Wanda, and it was at that point that, of her own volition, she sought to join him in therapy. Ten years after they terminated their therapy, Tom and Wanda are living a productive life together. They now appreciate — together — the blessings of four grandchildren.

Not all stories have the successful ending enjoyed by Tom and Wanda. Suppose you are one of those people who are not able to find anything good in your partner. I urge you not to give up. You may be projecting your own feelings of inadequacy. If you see your situation as hopeless, this may be your state of mind during a troublesome time. If you perceive your partner as an angry and stubborn individual, it may be that you, too, are angry and stubborn. Because this sort of perception is intolerable to you, you project it onto your partner. Simply, if you see yourself as a hammer, then your spouse or anyone else becomes a nail.

Suppose you take a positive approach and begin with what is at your fingertips. For example, say to yourself: "I'm alive. I have a mind and a functioning body. I can make decisions. I can move. I can be loving. I can do things that bring me satisfaction. I find joy in helping others. I will make a genuine effort to save whatever is worthwhile in my relationship. Life has a purpose. I'll take the first step to discover what my purpose in life is. Having identified my own strengths, I will try to appreciate my partner's strengths and find joy in our mutual participation in life."

To regain harmony, you need to consider that a relationship is an ongoing experience that needs encouragement. If you are looking for some sort of happy and productive coexistence, you need to facilitate the fulfillment of your partner. As you accept this person as the Very Important Person, the VIP in your life, your emotional self will be enriched with a great deal of joy. Visualize yourself sitting opposite your partner. Look into his or her eyes benevolently and appreciate the human mystery: a person with complex qualities, a person whom you have chosen to be your partner for life. As you look penetratingly into your partner's eyes, say, "This person is my VIP." Repeat this experience a few times and then proceed to treat your partner as your VIP. What a feeling! Try to enjoy it.

This type of exercise will give you the realization of acceptance. You have accepted someone significant into your life, giving that person the freedom to choose to grow or to stay put. Given such freedom and encouragement, the individual often chooses to move ahead and mature. More often than not, your partner will love you more and will allow you the same freedom. As you notice improvements in your relationship, you must be sure to show appreciation for positive changes. Better yet, you should plan to celebrate something good that you are experiencing. You could say, "It felt good when we worked on this chore together. Let's treat ourselves to a pleasant evening to celebrate our cooperation."

In failing to acknowledge progress, you discourage productive and mature interaction. Silence over something good that is happening in the relationship gives the impression that "nothing is good enough for you," or "I don't seem to do anything right," or "I don't seem to be able to please you." Lack of positive feedback breeds frustration or even passivity. Partners who do not receive any appreciation for their achievements, whether for the relationship or for personal accomplishments, feel discouraged or, indeed, ignored.

For example, when a partner comes home after a jogging experience and exuberantly exclaims, "I did two miles this morning!" and the other partner says, "It's about time you came back! I want some breakfast," it is a discouraging reply. It is more productive for harmony to say something like, "That's really great! Come and have a glass of juice with me; you must be thirsty," or "Jogging really energizes you; you look great!" Perhaps your partner enjoys caring for the garden and works hard weeding and planting. You may say, "Why are you wasting your time out there?" or "Those flowers are a delight; you've done a good job." You have choices regarding how you respond.

Encouragement skills require sensitivity and awareness of your partner's needs. Ask yourself what makes you partner tick? Why not encourage your partner? A happy and fulfilled person can unquestionably be a good partner. If one of the partners is ambitious or involved with many activities and the other is not, the less active partner must not be intimidated by the other's excitement. Instead, he or she can share the joy of the active partner. It is helpful to say, "I notice how happy and fulfilled you are. I am truly happy for you." It is poisonous to remark, "You're always involved; you have so many activities. But what about me?" You probably feel left out or excluded or even jealous. It is more effective to acknowledge the progress and then invite your partner to include an activity that might interest you. Otherwise, you will be left out, for no one can read your mind. "I would like to play tennis with you. I know I will enjoy both the game and the exercise," is more positive than saying, "You never ask me to play tennis with you." Of course, you can plan any activity that you like and invite your partner to participate.

The VIP concept is central to the new effort, for it promotes not only appreciation of each other's qualities but also respect. Your partner is the Very Important Person in your life. By respecting your partner's unique and irreplaceable character as a human being, you provide a climate that fosters self-esteem. If you convey to your partner the feeling, "I have faith in you; I know you are a very capable person; under the circumstances, you have made the right decision," in essence you are showing that you respect who your partner is and how your partner deals with life and living.

We cannot change our partners by our strong convictions, our wise advice and practical proposals, but we can offer a benevolent space where they feel encouraged and appreciated. In such a state of acceptance they may be able to listen with attention and care to a voice speaking to their hearts.

Sometimes it makes you feel good when you try to help by solving your partner's problem. If that's what you want to do — to be a troubleshooter for your partner — you should be aware of the results. You are encouraging dependency, and the day that you are not there to solve a problem, the interaction will be out of balance. A more effective way to help is to provide support. Believing in your partner's ability to handle a situation is a powerful contribution. Some individuals are helped most by being permitted to deal with a given situation with their own resources. Our support and trust in their ability to deal with a problem give a tremendous boost to our partner's self-image.

For Your Consideration

~ Make a date. Extend a loving invitation to your partner to meet in a mutually agreed upon place. Breakfast, lunch, dinner, or simply a stroll in the nearest park is a good start. Make it as inviting as you did when you were dating.

~ Thank your partner for accepting the invitation. This gives you both a warm feeling and helps to animate the relationship.

~ Promise yourself that you will not get into anything negative that will disturb the experience. Listen attentively to what your partner has to say and respond with a sentence that begins with "You" instead of "I."

~ Resist the need to boast about yourself. Strive to be interested in the life of your partner rather than trying to make an impression. Show that you care to hear about the accomplishments of the other.

~ When you feel distant, unable to make a connection with your partner, pick one of the sentences below and complete it with a compliment:

> ~ I feel good being here with you because . . .

> ~ I appreciate it when . . .

> ~ One thing I admire about you is. . . .

~ Talk about experiences that made your relationship special.

~ Recall a favorite event that you both enjoyed and suggest that you visit the place where it occurred. Talk about a romantic experience you remember.

~ Propose an activity that you will plan for both of you.

Chapter 3

THE CONCEPT OF CHANGE

All changes, even the most longed for, have their melancholy;
for what we leave behind us is a part of ourselves; we must
die to one life before we can enter into another.
                                                — ANATOLE FRANCE

During the first few years of Adam and Carol's marriage, buying and decorating a house kept them busy on weekends, and periodically they rewarded themselves with a champagne dinner at a fancy restaurant, an activity they both enjoyed.

For some time, the interaction between Carol and Adam as partners remained unchanged and unchallenged, but eventually it ceased to engender delight, zest, or growth. Adam and Carol failed to notice that their relationship was going through phases. The bond that held them together changed as circumstances changed.

Eventually, familiarity became boring. Exhausted after their day's work, they went to bed where, night after night, they either watched television or read. Gradually both of them became bored with such a relationship; they were distant, trite, suffocating. Each morning, they reentered this meaningless existence. They ate a scanty breakfast, gave each other a peck on the cheek, and dashed away in different directions to their jobs. Familiar?

When the arrangement of the living-room furniture began to pall, Carol shuffled things around until the new decor pleased her. Adam was oblivious to the changes. It did not matter to him which way the furniture faced or which painting hung on which wall. On weekends he was seldom around. Dissatisfied with the local golf course, he flew to Arizona or Florida for a game of golf with his friends.

What had happened to love and passion? The early stages

of romance evolved into a passion for success and status. They both became immersed in making money. Adam worked ungodly hours as a stockbroker; Carol, an insurance representative, had a demanding position that involved traveling out of state.

On one of her travels, a male associate admired her spirit and paid extra attention to her presentations. Enamored by the charms of this man, she felt unsettled. When she returned home, Adam was not around. She decided to take a bubble bath and unwind. The water was soothing, and as she relaxed, indulging in pleasant fantasies, she thought of her out-of-town associate. He had been most attentive. He made her laugh. She told herself that Adam would not care; he was busy with new clients, and she had been far from home with time on her hands. She talked herself into believing that for certain emotional needs she would look outside her marriage. Her thoughts evolved into a fantasy: "There are men out there who could make me happy. Maybe I married the wrong person." When Adam came home that night, he found Carol distant and preoccupied. Maybe she's tired, he thought. And after some surface talk he drifted into the next room and turned on his computer to surf the internet.

Adam and Carol, married for five years, sought marital counseling because they had lost the initial fervor of passion that had propelled them into marriage. I agreed to see them on a Sunday evening because they were worn out from arguing and had decided to see a lawyer on Monday morning to begin divorce proceedings. "He has become a workaholic," she claimed, "and has no time for me." His complaint was that Carol nagged and wanted to control him. Both looked disappointed; they were bogged down in a state of emotional paralysis and were skeptical about the survival of their relationship. After a fiery two-hour session, they agreed to delay calling their attorneys. Even though there were huge hurdles to overcome, once they had ventilated their anger, they admitted to me that they wanted to preserve their marriage. I reassured them that it could be done if they were willing to work harder than they ever had to resolve the conflicts.

After a moment's reflection, you may realize that Adam and Carol had accepted a static concept of marriage, and by doing so they had diminished their power to use capacities for growth and improvement to good purpose in other areas of their lives. Was there a way to give their relationship the care it needed, to make sure that each one got the kind of response that enables growth, to pursue a partnership that promotes good will and joy?

A relationship is a living, flexible, growing thing, much like a green plant that pops out from a tiny seed and gradually becomes a huge vine. It is never the same for very long; it needs feeding and pruning, different kinds and amounts of nurturing and caring at different times. When couples do not have a mental picture of their relationship as a living entity outside themselves — an entity that, like a plant, needs shaping and nourishment at every stage of development — then they are apt to neglect each other's needs.

After months of diligent work, their marriage finally stabilized. Adam and Carol admitted that they no longer believed divorce was the answer to their turbulent marriage, and they no longer wished to seek legal advice. After a personal inventory and consideration of conflicted areas, they realized that they had succumbed to a static relationship, tolerating self-complacency and defeat. They had reached the stage where they were determined to honestly explore what each one of them needed to do about the areas of concern.

In one of her visits to my office, Carol acknowledged regrets with regard to her fantasies. In her own words:

> This other man, my out-of-town associate, was very wealthy, charming, and generous. He said he would give me anything I wanted if I decided to leave my husband, and I almost fell for his offer. It was a terrible thought to consider such a proposition. I must have been nuts. I was not after wealth. All I needed was some extra attention, intimacy, which I didn't have at home. Then it dawned on me that I was capable of getting it. My husband is a good man, good natured, generous, and ambitious. All I need to do is to change my approach and be more available to him. First, I must learn to give Adam what I expect him to give me. I need to focus more on Adam's needs and make an effort to fulfill his expectations of me as well as I can. Second, I need to be more caring about my interaction with Adam and less obsessive about my work.

In the next session, Carol told me about a meeting she initiated with her boss. She told him that her marriage was her first priority and that therefore, it was important for her to limit her out-of-town travel. Fortunately her boss understood and reduced the frequency of her travels. In the ensuing three months, Carol and Adam made a concerted effort to deal with obstacles that appeared to be destructive. Adam slowed down considerably and came home earlier. He limited his nights out and dedicated Thursday evenings to Carol. For about six weeks they came to my office for marital counseling. Each time, they brought a list of issues that needed attention. We dealt with what seemed most important at the time. For example, Carol wanted every Thursday to be their night together. Adam thought it was a good idea, provided they did not deal with grievances that night. Carol said, "We'll plan a fun time together." They made a commitment that at six o'clock on Thursday evenings they would get together for their RT (Royal Treatment) time.

The RT experiences brought them closer, and they looked forward to every Thursday, when they could unwind and enjoy the evening. They talked to each other with respect, and as they became more confident about their marriage, they appropriated a Saturday morning to deal with issues pertinent to their life together.

Carol and Adam found the following skills productive:

1. Treat the other person with respect.
   You are seeking solution for a mutual issue. As the other person initiates discussion, listen attentively. Allow the other to finish the thought. Do not interrupt. Respect the new direction of your relationship.

2. Treat the other person with awareness.
   You want a viable solution to whatever problem you are facing. The solution to any problem can be productive if both partners participate in finding the answer. The way you listen or look at the other person, the tone of voice, the selection of words — all contribute toward a solution.

3. Treat the other with acceptance.
   You may find that the opinions held by you and your partner on the same issue are different. Accept the opinions of the

other, not as right or wrong, but as different. "I'm right and you're wrong" does not solve a problem. It causes distance.

4. Table the discussion.
   When a dialogue becomes heated and leads to an impasse, a wise way to go is to say, "We have reached a point where further conversation on the subject would make matters worse. Let's table this discussion until we gain a better understanding of the problem."

5. Agree to disagree.
   In any relationship a conflict may remain unsolved for a long time. Couples who desire to stay together need to say to each other: "Let's be courteous to each other and caring of each other until we find a satisfactory answer to our problem."

Applying the above guide, Carol and Adam rediscovered their potential as partners. As they experienced the joy of working together, they enhanced the guidelines with their own insight. Gradually their ability to solve problems improved, and their marital life took a favorable turn.

Far from being the perfect couple, now and then they experience periods of frustration with each other, but they have learned new skills of communication. A deeper love binds them together, which enables them to make the needed changes and to work through problems.

Kindle New Hope

Changing your behavior in your relationship requires an investment of time, energy, and effort. It may involve some discomfort and even pain. Change is always fraught with risk. Whenever you try to change some aspect of your life, you feel uncertain or even vulnerable. But growing up and maturing involve changing. To resist change is to arrest development.

For example, in order to grow, the lobster has to shed its shell many times. Each time it sheds, the creature is totally defenseless until the new shell forms. Nature teaches us this lesson in many different ways. It is no different with us: from infancy to adulthood, every phase of life demands change. You need to have faith that change will lead to improvement in the relationship, which will bring rewards to you and to your partner. These rewards must, in fact, be forthcoming if you are to keep up the changed behavior.

If you do not believe that there is a potential for growth in your relationship, then all of the above is quite irrelevant, because your mind will be closed to the possibility that something much better is, in fact, available to you if only you would stir yourself to action. I believe that when you find ways to kindle new hope in your relationship, you will discover the potential of a much more satisfying and rewarding experience.

In nine out of ten couples who seek marital therapy, one spouse wants the other to change. "Change into what?" the other protests. "There is nothing wrong with me or with our marriage. It's you who may need to change."

Most therapists will tell you that you cannot change the world except to the extent you can change yourself. You cannot change other people. They are as they are. You can change yourself, however, *only* to the degree you alter, modify, or become aware of your unrealistic expectations of what-should-be. It is the what-should-be that bars the gate to reality. You and you alone can change your life. If you do so, you may have a positive influence on another person, who may begin to like or even emulate your behavior.

One of the quickest and most dramatic ways to improve any significant relationship is for the partners to change, not each other, but their own *behavior* toward each other. This change can happen only if the necessary conditions are met. To create favorable conditions for any meaningful change, awareness and vigilance are two important criteria.

Awareness: The biggest single gift you can give to yourself during a lifetime does not come in a pretty box or fancy wrappings. It does not cost a lot of money, and it may never impress the neighbors. It's a quiet, readily available commodity known as self-awareness, and although it cannot be acquired without an expenditure of time and effort, it will pay handsome dividends.

The idea of awareness presents us with a hopeful sign. An increasing number of couples, groups, and individuals work diligently to attain a harmonious life. On many levels in our daily experiences, living with another person and working with other people, we are discovering that we *can* make a difference in the quality of life in our society. By freely choosing to give of ourselves, our time, energy, and talent, we find that we grow richer and feel happier and that our lives are more satisfactory.

Vigilance: This is a good word to remember. Being vigilant of your thoughts, feelings, and actions will provide a healthy attitude toward your life. Regrets, recriminations, and alibis based on your past experiences are no longer significant; their purpose is to serve as lessons.

The here-and-now concept may be of comfort to you. Life is being. And all being is now. Your life can be neither postponed nor transposed. Alienation from your present reality, your current situation with your partner, is emotionally disturbing — a flight from reality into dreams and fantasy. But you do have a choice. Either you live in direct, spontaneous contact with the emerging *now* and respond to your current situation with a sense of pride, responsibility, and gratitude for what is available to you, or you live fearfully on the deferred payment plan as an alien from reality in a world of inertia and wishful thinking. There is no middle road; there are no shades of gray.

If you find this a reasonable position from which to start — that is, exploring and refining your thoughts, taking serious charge of your positive qualities — then you are ready for action. A word of caution: In the presence of your partner, watch your restless heart, watch the mercurial way your mind sweeps from one thing to another. Observe your expectations and avoid criticizing, comparing, competing. Suspend judgment and evaluation. Notice how physically close you can be with your partner, and yet how unavailable you may be on a deeper level. Practice receiving the other with the whole of your heart, being fully present with an attentive ear and a receptive mind.

Of course you must be motivated to initiate change; the motivation comes from a strong conviction that change is possible. Once you have acted to initiate the desired change, you must be sufficiently rewarded to go on repeating the healthier behavior pattern until it has been firmly established. It takes careful planning to provide these conditions. Information on how to do things may be worthwhile, but what you need even more is the sensitive application of healthier behavior.

After forty-four years of observation, I have come to realize that very few marriages, perhaps from 5 to 10 percent, function at a really high level of mutual satisfaction. This conclusion may sound somewhat pessimistic or even depressing. It implies that 90 percent of marital relationships are not in very good shape. But it does not help to explain the widespread dissatisfaction with marriage today, which, of course, is a function of our higher expectations of ourselves and of our spouses. Volumes can be written on reasons why marriages fail.

What is most important here is that your relationship could reach a far higher level of satisfaction if you could be helped to realize your potential. A remark attributed to Albert Einstein states that most of us go through life without using more than about 10 percent of our intellectual potential. This concept suggests that most of us likewise go through life with a mere fraction of our capacity for love and companionship either realized or expressed. We take each other for granted.

You may agree with me that a relationship cannot remain static. A living entity as unique as the persons who share it, a relationship can be developed and enhanced to meet the emerging needs of the partners. Both you and your partner have a latent capacity and a desperate need to give and receive love. Often this capacity has been inhibited and restrained by cultural pressures; yet it can stir and awaken and come alive when the right conditions are created. By now you are beginning to discover how these conditions can be manifested.

You will be impressed with the results once you make the decision to maintain your relationship, not the old static relationship but the remodeled one, the one that you want to share with your partner.

Now that you have made a decisive step, the next step is to pinpoint areas of adjustment for improvement.

In their book *We Can Have Better Marriages*, David and Vera Mace propose the following. You and your partner:

1. decide on common goals and values

2. make a commitment to growth

3. use communication skills

4. deal with conflict creatively

5. demonstrate appreciation and affection

6. agree on gender roles

7. cooperate and work as a team

8. give each other sexual fulfillment

9. work together on managing your money

10. discuss aspects of parenting

As you review the above items, feel free to add your own areas of concern. Visualize what your interaction would be like if you were to develop it fully. This means that you would have to tune in to this aspect of your relationship, sincerely and diligently together, learning all you could about each other, seeking all the help you could command, making all the progress of which you are capable. This effort would represent your full human potential in this area, according to your best evaluation. At this point, pause for a moment. Look at your present relationship and consider how much progress you have already made toward realizing its potential. Be honest about it, but also be fair to yourself.

Maturity occurs slowly. You can transcend yourself only in spurts. You are the architect of your life. As you redesign it, include the possibility of a better relationship. Talk to a friend whose relationship you admire and discuss what it takes to be an effective partner.

In the next encounter with your partner, bring what you perceive as improvement and discuss it for at least twenty minutes together, sharing what you think is happening. Allow this to be your initiative, with which your partner may or may not agree. Further, if there is a disagreement, discuss it with the assumption that each person is entitled to his or her own perception. It is okay to agree to disagree. It is still progress. The objective here is not to find out what is wrong with your relationship, but to rediscover its unclaimed potential. This discovery is very exciting, like discovering a lot of money that you had stashed but forgotten in the bottom of your drawer.

There is a simplicity about this process, which I warmly invite you to try out yourself. It has proved helpful to many couples in opening their minds to the possibility and the reality of growth.

Reassess Your Needs

At times, external coercions — resulting from our developing technology, constant mobility, disturbing demands at work, competitive comparisons with others, social pressures, public opinion — hinder personal as well as interpersonal growth. But because we are seeking fulfillment and happiness, we have no other choice but to delve realistically into the core of the matter and learn what our needs are. We may not get all that we want from our partner — nobody does — but can we strike a viable balance so that both partners feel rewarded as their needs are being met?

In his bestselling book *His Needs, Her Needs,* Willard E. Harley, Jr., points out five basic needs men expect their wives to fulfill, and five needs women want their husbands to meet. Let's take a look at them.

Men want:

1. sexual fulfillment

2. recreational companionship

3. an attractive spouse

4. domestic support (a well-maintained, peaceful home)

5. admiration (that is, "respect")

Women want:

1. affection

2. conversation

3. honesty and openness

4. financial support

5. family commitment

Marriage therapists find that Harley's lists touch on nerve centers that cause the most trouble in marriage. We might describe some of these needs in different terms, but in essence, these needs, regardless of each one's weight, are common to both men and women, and seek fulfillment.

Bestselling author Dr. Kevin Leman believes that husbands and wives can do a lot to strengthen their marriages if they honestly confront both the man's need for sexual fulfillment and the woman's need for affection. At a seminar, a woman challenged him: "Are you trying to say that men like sex and women don't? Are you trying to say that women only want affection?"

He responded, "Not at all. I believe that when a man shows a woman the right kind of affection, it prepares her to enjoy tremendous sex. Many women can enjoy sex to a higher degree than men."

Sexuality and attention for both husband and wife are very important ingredients for a good marriage. They go hand in hand; you cannot have one without the other. However, we know well that it takes more to maintain and develop a relationship. It takes respect and the ability to see your partner not as a man or not as a woman but as a person, not as an object that can fulfill your needs. Marriage, like a pie, consists of several pieces. In addition to love, sexuality, attention, and respect, there are other parts, including the following:

1. Expectations. Marriage is an opportunity to share life with another human being. This is truly one of life's greatest gifts. What really damages and bruises this gift are our high expectations. The higher your expectation, the more difficult your interaction with each other will be.

2. Communications. The patterns of communication that you learned earlier in your home of origin affect and continue to affect your married life. As you interact with your partner, it is important to observe what is good and works with your partner. Leave behind you what is hazardous and destructive.

3. Resolving conflicts. To presume that you and your partner will go through life without disagreements or arguments is idealistic, even naive. Be careful not to make the disagreement or argument into a contest where one wins and the other loses. Let the relationship be the winner.

4. Money. After sex, money is the major contributory factor to discord. Often a dispute over money is symptomatic of deeper emotional problems, either individual or shared. If you have

problems managing your money, you may need professional guidance from a financial consultant.

5. Time together. Time management may be defined as the art of planning your time to fulfill your goals. Regardless of what your priorities are, if you do not appropriate time to be with your partner, ultimately your relationship will be endangered. You need time together when you can be physically and emotionally available to each other. Once you learn to enjoy quality time together, the next choice may be to network with other couples whose company you would find interesting.

Many are the pieces of the pie, and each one needs to be handled with care and respect. What will keep each piece intact for your personal enjoyment is your daily dialogue. A fifteen-to-twenty-minute dialogue a day is to your relationship what blood is to your body. When the flow of blood stops, the body dies. When the dialogue stops, the relationship withers, and resentment and disappointment are born.

In your earnest efforts to bring about a change in your relationship, the next time you meet your partner propose the following exercise. It will take only a few precious minutes of focusing on the other. It is a structured dialogue that promises results — a more harmonious relationship — if you are both willing to participate. A couple told me recently that for an entire week, morning and evening, they practiced this exercise, and it dramatically changed their interaction.

Try to relax your mind and entertain certain concepts as being possible. With a sincere desire and intention to be open to possible change, sit across from each other as if you were to touch knees. Touch knees, if both feel comfortable about touching. The important thing is that you look into each other's eyes, possibly with a smile. Now, start reading the paragraphs that follow, slowly and distinctly. It matters not who starts first. The one who listens has to repeat the same paragraph slowly and distinctly. It is very important that each statement is addressed by each partner individually. Take your time and let the dialogue flow:

Partner A: You, [John], and I have a relationship that I value and want to develop and maintain. Yet, each of us is a separate person with unique needs and desires, and you have every right to have yours fulfilled.

(Partner B repeats the above)

Partner B: When you, [Christine], are having problems meeting your needs, I will listen with genuine empathy and acceptance in order to help you arrive at your own solutions, instead of depending on mine. I respect your right to choose your own beliefs and develop your own values although they may differ from mine.

(Partner A repeats the above)

Partner A: When your behavior interferes with what I must do to meet my own needs, I will tell you openly and honestly how your behavior affects me. I trust that you will respect my needs and feelings enough to change behavior that is unacceptable to me. Whenever my behavior is unacceptable to you, I want you to tell me openly and honestly so that I can change my behavior accordingly.

(Partner B repeats the above)

Partner B: If we both realize that one of us cannot change to meet the other's needs, we have to acknowledge that we have a conflict. This may be a good place to stop and consider what the conflict is telling us about ourselves. It might even give us a new direction. However, it is important that we commit ourselves to resolving the conflict without resorting to the use of power or manipulation to *win* at the expense of the other *losing*.

(Partner A repeats the above)

Partner A: I respect your needs, but I also respect my own. I will appreciate it when you are able to meet some of my needs. I do not expect you to fulfill all my needs; that is my responsibility. Together we must seek fulfillment of our needs and provide solutions to our problems.

(Partner B repeats the above)

Partner B: In this way, you can continue to develop as a person, and so can I. Ours can be a healthy relationship in which both of us strive to become what we are capable of being. We can continue to relate to each other with mutual respect, love, and understanding.

(Partner A repeats the above)

Partner A: The man-woman relationship is the most personal, deepest, and potentially most beautiful relationship two human beings can have. In the days to come, I will make it my task to safeguard what we have started with faith and trust in each other's potential. I will honestly tune in to your needs and strive to attain a better relationship with you. This I promise.

(Partner B repeats the above)

In recent years, most people have become aware of the benefit of physical exercise. Millions of dollars have been invested in physical fitness centers and self-help gadgets that promote physical health. The secret to all means of exercise is regularity and repetition. No exercise of any sort can be of benefit if it is not systematically and regularly repeated. This is also true of emotional fitness and improvement of relationships.

This exercise, as well as other points proposed in this book, will have little or no effect on your life if they are not repeated and practiced regularly.

~ TWO ~

DISPENSE YOUR ANGER WISELY

If you dispense anger wisely,
it can be a creative energy.
If you let it lurk in your heart,
anger causes both emotional and physical damage.

⸎

Ask your partner for help with your anger.

Chapter 4

A MULTIFACETED EMOTION

He that is slow to anger is better than the mighty.
— PROVERBS 16:32

The ways we deal with our angry feelings dictate the degree of strength and potential survival of our relationships. Many professionals agree that the main cause of the breakup of relationships is rooted in anger: couples do not know how to handle their anger toward each other. The mismanagement of anger is one of the greatest social problems today. Spouses are verbally and physically abused, and children are aggressively injured; verbal and physical attacks occur as a result of mismanaged anger. Our quality of life depends greatly on the state of our mind; there can be no inner peace and fulfillment unless we bridle and resolve this powerful innate emotion.

What is anger? Anger may be defined as a sudden, keen displeasure aroused by real or assumed injury or injustice; it is usually accompanied by the desire to punish. Anger, with its own ramifications — annoyance, frustration, fury, irritation, indignation, rage, revenge — darkens the mind and is detrimental to a person's development. In relationships, particularly in marriage, anger can become catastrophic if it is not observed and dispelled wisely. It is a major obstacle in human interaction.

Cheryl stormed out of her house one evening with her two children, determined not to return to her husband. What would cause a person to take such a drastic action? "I've had it with him. I'm furious. I don't want to see him ever again," she ranted. On her way to the neighboring town where her parents lived, she speculated that if she and her children stayed with them for about three months, she could save enough money to get her own apartment. Nervously, she smiled at the prospect and whispered, "Free at last."

Cheryl and Steven had been married for eleven years. Initially they had decided not have children, but they did want love and intimacy, and within a few years, in spite of their original intention, they were parents of two baby girls. Cheryl and Steven both worked hard and sought to secure material possessions, including a comfortable home. But as they moved closer to each other, something happened. Differences between them, which seemed unimportant or even attractive during their two years of courtship, became threatening and precipitated arguments. Their dialogue included such remarks as, "You make me laugh. Come on now, don't act the martyr."

"We need to visit my parents this week. Mother would like to see her grandchildren more often," said Cheryl.

"Look, what do you want from me? I'm under a lot of pressure. I can't drop everything and run every time your mother speaks," replied Steven.

"Just forget it, will you, please? Just pretend I never said it, and let's drop the whole thing, okay?" she said.

"You're a pain in the neck."

"Man, you're no ray of sunshine!"

In time, Cheryl and Steven, in a more direct and unguarded manner, used additional poignant expressions of anger in their daily interaction — and this drove them further apart. Each felt cheated; marriage did not give them what they had expected. They began sleeping in separate rooms. Love-making ceased, and since they could no longer communicate without a major disagreement, they relinquished their quest for any sort of intimacy with each other. Cheryl found some relief in divulging her marital dissatisfaction to a male colleague who had abandoned his wife and two children and was rooming with a male friend. Misery needs company; Cheryl and her newly found confidant had a lot in common, and they did their best to comfort each other. Cheryl's underlying thoughts — "Where have you been all my life? You're such a nice man! If you could only be mine" — deepened the rift between herself and her husband. She made up her mind that she no longer loved Steven; she wanted a divorce. Steven, having seen the writing on the wall, reached a similar conclusion that their marriage had been a grave mistake.

Cheryl stayed with her parents for about six weeks, and when she found a more lucrative job, she got her own apartment and began the life of a single woman. Contrary to her parents' admonitions and her husband's requests that she return to her home and give their marriage another chance, Cheryl retained a lawyer and started divorce proceedings.

After the divorce, Steven went to a therapist, who helped him understand his contribution to the failure of the marriage. This was Steven's second marriage failure. When he walked away from his first marriage, he mercilessly blamed his wife for her lack of understanding and her constant nagging. Therapy helped him realize and overcome the deep bitterness he felt toward women in general. His mother had died when he was an infant. Lurking in his subconscious was a child's perception: "My mother left me. She betrayed me. Women are not to be trusted." This unrecognized anger caused him to keep women at a distance. Each time he moved closer to Cheryl, seeking her affection, anger flared and consumed his loving feelings. Did Steven know the origin of his anger? In therapy, he became aware that his angry feelings toward Cheryl had very little to do with what she did or said. His anger was the result of damaged emotions that he had experienced since the tragic loss of his mother. It is true that sometimes a debilitating anger starts in childhood, either with some significant loss or some sort of serious abuse. Gradually Steven became aware that he also expressed anger toward his wife in covert and passive ways, with silence, sarcasm, criticism, and humor in poor taste, unconsciously staging another loss in his life.

More marriages today are dying from silence than from violence. When Steven did not get his way, he repressed his anger and resorted to silence. His coldness and unexpressed hostility were unhealthy ways used to get revenge on his wife. "I need to know what you're angry about," Cheryl insisted. "I can't deal with your silence. I can't read minds."

Marriage probably generates more anger in the average man or woman than any other social situation in which they are involved. Although a large number of couples manage to suppress their real feelings, confidential files of family therapists are inundated with accounts of battered wives, battered children, and even battered husbands. However, despite all this battering and all the mental and physical abuse in the family system, there is in our society a large number of wives, and a fair number of husbands too, who suppress their anger — they choke it down, swallow it, keep it under control — until they finally reach the point at which it is not only hidden from outside observers, but hidden also from their own partners, and even from themselves. Consciously, to avoid an explosion, they pretend that everything is just fine. Then one day, there is an outburst of anger; an explosive argument occurs over something insignificant, causing turmoil or even destruction. Emerging from the depths of the subconscious mind, past hurts and unresolved issues surface. War is declared.

Sometimes the partners act out; they take off; and don't want to be married any more. Others go out and have an affair to pun-ish-their partner or to prove to themselves that someone out there could love them more than their spouse does. Cheryl, in her search for someone who would love and appreciate her more than Steven did, became emotionally and physically involved with her con-fidant, her colleague at work. He assured her he was planning a divorce, but after a year of their passionate affair and many promises, her danceaway lover decided to return to his wife and children. Cheryl, in despair and with a broken heart, wished she had stayed with Steven and worked things out.

Some couples, unable to deal with each other's angry feelings, develop a defensive relationship, engaging in a power struggle where each one strives to gain ascendancy over the other. Nei-ther is willing to see the other's needs; neither is willing to respect and accept the other as a unique person with unique qualities and aspirations. They keep their distance, they await the next argu-ment, they deny they are in the wrong. Usually both are partially wrong; but for one to admit being wrong is to run the risk of ad-mitting that the other is right. Such an attitude is fruitless. They may decide to stay married for many years in the hope that some-thing will change for the better, but at the same time they maintain their "war of the roses," which inevitably results in the death of a relationship.

When Your Needs Are Not Met

Can anger really destroy a relationship? If it is not dealt with properly, it surely can. Many relationships have been destroyed because of unresolved anger. Where does this anger come from? When needs are not met, people get angry with each other. For reasons of their own, some individuals are angry with themselves. Either they feel less accomplished or they feel that they didn't get out of life what they really wanted. They feel that, in some way, parents, life, society, or circumstances have deprived them of what they deserved. They bring frustration and anger into their encounters, which the romantic period tends to diffuse. But two angry individuals make an angry relationship.

Angry feelings need to be talked about when they occur. Responsible partners face their anger with care and sensitivity to avoid causing irreparable damage to their relationship. The childish desire to get even with the wrongdoer at once lowers the aggressor to the plane of his or her opponent, feeding the immature natures of both and poisoning the relationship. The nature of revenge, whether mild or intense, is to wreak vengeance directly upon its victims. In a marital relationship, revenge is the poison that brings about slow death to the partnership.

As with all of our emotions, there is nothing wrong with anger in its proper place, for a proper cause. Anger is our human response to something wrong or unjust that occurs, or that we perceive to have occurred. Anger can be a good emotion. When we hear about or see an injustice, when we witness the violation of someone's property, when someone wrongs us, our anger motivates us to take appropriate action. Anger can be a good emotion when it gets us moving, but if we let it fester inside us, we set ourselves up for a great deal of potential harm.

In important relationships such as marriage, all those little discussions that do not seem to get resolved and periodically provoke inappropriate outbursts are usually driven by anger simmering just below the surface:

"The house looks like a pigsty."

"You never do anything around the house."

"I'm not your maid."

"You're always on the phone talking to your friends."

"If you were not so lazy, you'd pick up a brush and paint the garage."

The list can be endless, and the anger can keep the couple apart and in turmoil.

Most troubles in managing anger in marriage today arise from the fact that the average couple knows of only three ways to deal with anger: to ignore it, to vent it, or to suppress it. There can be little progress if the partners do not learn how to process their angry feelings.

When we ignore anger or walk away from it, as practical as it may appear, the emotion follows us. And the next time we get angry because we cannot get what we want or need, our anger comes out in full force, and it can wreak havoc.

It has been a popular concept that venting anger, getting it out of your system, is healthy. Is it? Some people periodically lose their tempers and quickly return to normal. Others hold anger in or explode beyond the point of immediate relief, but they do not get rid of their angry feelings. They remain in a state of tension and walk around like time bombs. Venting anger needs to be done with consideration of the other person. Specify the issue or the event that you are angry about and focus on it. For example, your partner promises to be home at seven o'clock for dinner, but doesn't arrive until nine. Instead of saying, "You are rude and inconsiderate," you should say, "I'm really angry that you did not even make a phone call and tell me about the delay." In this case, the anger is focused on the delay, and thus the person is not under attack.

When you find yourself in a situation where venting your anger could result in violence, it is of great benefit to suppress the violent urge. Although the initial waves of anger may be beyond your control, try to exercise reason. Follow the old axiom: When you get angry, count to ten; if you are very angry count to one hundred. This allows your anger a few moments to subside, and then you can deal with troublesome issues more productively.

We respond angrily when something hurtful happens to us that is outside our control. It is a normal response, even a good response. Although we can choose to hold on to anger, like a defense weapon threatening whoever has hurt us, it is better to drop the threatening weapon. Simply let go of the anger and dare to reason.

Especially in a marital relationship, anger should not be welcomed into our heart as a guest into our home. When we allow angry feelings to linger and settle in, they bring harm not only to ourselves and to our partner but also to our relationship. Trace these feelings — where do they originate? It's easy to blame someone else for feeling the way we do. Does another person really have such power over us?

Just think of all the times you have felt frustrated, hurt, or fearful. Is it your practice to ignore, vent, or suppress such feelings, or to face them gently and, with the sensitivity of a wise surgeon, try to remove them as if they were malignant tumors? This is a better option.

Chapter 5

THE ORIGINS OF ANGER

Most fits of anger or touchiness are but an expression of a feeling of insecurity, inferiority or a sense of false pride. Anger represents a very intimate interaction between the mind and the body. — THURMAN FLEET

Have you ever exploded angrily at someone who somehow wronged you? Was this person close to you? Do you recall how you felt as you attacked that person verbally or perhaps even physically? Do you remember your heart pounding, your neck veins swelling, your blood throbbing in your temples? As you think back, do you sense a lingering angry feeling about that incident still gnawing within you?

If we take a deeper look at one of our angry episodes, we might discover that the intensity of our anger could be called into question. Did we really need to get so upset? Was it worth it? What did we really accomplish?

Something contrary to your wishes occurs. You have an instant reaction. When your angry reaction suddenly connects with anger existing within and is fueled, you have a tantrum. When the anger subsides, you wonder how you could have been so angry, especially with a loved one. Do you sense a tinge of guilt?

Thirty-six-year-old Richard grew furious at his widowed mother when he discovered that she had started dating. Confronting her with his anger would have jeopardized their relationship on which he was dependent. He did have strong feelings for his mother; when his father died ten years before, Richard replaced him as head of the household. Unconsciously, he displaced his anger in a curious way. He began dating older women as potential wives — shall we say mother substitutes? Invariably, these alliances went sour each time the relationship became intimate, and he found himself attacking the women angrily of the slightest pretext. In therapy he realized gradually that his real anger was against his mother, but fear of the jealousy he harbored made him turn his fury against other women of her age.

When you sense excessive irritability and you find yourself attacking people, wanting to punish the slightest offense, perhaps an inner inventory might help you. Why am I so angry? Eventually you may realize whatever the crime was, it did not merit such anger. At best, you apologize and feel better when the matter is clarified and the relationship is restored.

As we consider the results of our angry behavior with a cooler mind, we can trace the real origins of our anger. Actually it begins the moment life begins. During gestation, the fetus knows only the safety of the womb where the mother's body provides for every aspect of growth. The mother manufactures its food, supplies life-sustaining oxygen, and maintains delicate climatic controls; she nourishes and protects. It is a sort of ideal room service. When the infant emerges into a suddenly hostile world, it must gasp for the breath of life; it knows cold and hunger and pain for the first time; it experiences a brutal shock. At first, the mother still sees to the infant's primary needs and provides emotional as well as physical satisfactions. As soon as some basic want goes unmet, that tiny, helpless bundle squalls angrily for attention. Having been secure at the center of its own little universe, instinctively the infant protests being thrust into an alien world.

Far from being fanciful, the feeling persists in all of us through early life that we, as children, are the center of the world. One of the more difficult adjustments we make in growing up is accepting the fact that we are not the axis around which all things and all people revolve. We soon discover that there are other people who are interested in themselves and not particularly or exclusively concerned with us. For some individuals who do not learn this fact of life early enough or well enough, infantile anger persists. They walk into the world, as the cliché puts it, with a chip on their shoulder, irritable and dissatisfied with life.

As children grow and are no longer regarded as completely helpless, responsibility begins to be thrust upon them. Total and uninhibited freedom begins to find restriction. Mother and father begin to have expectations. Abridgements of freedom, from toilet training to eating with an implement, lie at every step. Frustration or anger are either ignored or met with a stern "No!" The parental role, at least initially, is to make the child acceptable to society.

Did you understand this process when you were a baby? Do you recall having a temper tantrum, holding your breath until your mother was absolutely terrified? Maybe you didn't have temper tantrums, perhaps you cried a great deal when you did not get your way. Unlike adults who normally cry in pain or sorrow, children cry in anger most of the time. But they also adjust to their normal daily frustrations in play, even as adults do.

Before long, children learn to articulate their anger in fairly direct terms: "I hate you!" "I wish you were dead!" This is not some malevolent speaking dwarf. It is a frustrated or resentful child saying to a parent, "I'm angry with you." Unarticulated, children's anger may be vented in the destruction of their own or, more likely, a sibling's toys or a parent's furniture or books. It is neither unusual nor abnormal for youngsters to torment younger children or animals.

School tends to become the principal arena for destructive and constructive anger to compete. Children dissipate considerable angry energy in the acquisition of skills and knowledge. As they compete vigorously to succeed, to excel, to be noticed, their angry energy results in fights and hostile behavior. Though the anger may very well be toward parents, it is often unconsciously transferred to teachers, who may be unaware of the transfer.

Who would ever imagine that a handsome, intelligent, and seemingly decent schoolboy would plot, plan, pick up a gun, and kill his classmates? We may still wonder what evil forces linger in the mind of a serial murderer or what prompts the polite and tidy babysitter to kill an infant. We can reasonably assume that catastrophes occur when the unbridled and unresolved emotion of anger remains unattended in its early stages.

With the onset of adolescence come the really turbulent years. On the one hand, adolescents rebel against authority that persists in treating them as children; on the other hand, they resent the lifting of parental protection, which remains necessary. Adolescents are caught up in a classic double-bind: they want to be independent, and they also want to be taken care of. They are frustrated, and their anger is nurtured.

Mr. Stern could not strike a viable balance. Turning angrily toward his daughter Cindy, he said, "You want to be independent? Fine! But don't come whining to me."

"Dad, you're rude."

Cindy felt abandoned, misunderstood, and angry. Her father's attitude, perhaps rhetorical, shattered her confidence and brought a fierce conflict between her need to be dependent and her growing need to be herself. Realizing that she needed a home to live in and parental support to go to college, she resorted to external compliance and seething silence. Her father, viewing Cindy as a moody teenager, added, "If you expect to live in this house, you're going to have to abide by my rules."

How many tragic runaways have acted out of anger against such an uncompromising threat to their "personhood"?

Since total independence is an unattainable illusion, a more practical and productive approach in dealing with conflicted areas is an effort to negotiate. When parents and adolescents learn to negotiate, they may both discover realistic guidelines for gradual and healthy interdependence and self-reliance. Meanwhile, there will be parental understanding, the kind that pulls on the tether only when the mutually agreed upon limits have been exceeded.

In terms of our natural anger, as we emerge from adolescence and we mature, we begin to find, and consciously pursue, more constructive outlets: schooling beyond what is mandatory, work, sports, planning and fashioning a career. In short, we establish ourselves as independent individuals in society, successful and fulfilled in the field of our choice, recognized and respected.

If you are still asking why we get so angry, the answer lies in the fact that life itself often disappoints most of us. Our deep primitive wish is to have things our way, to be taken care of, to be the center of our world, to have power over things and over people that oppose us, to be perfect. Of course none of this is really possible, but our instincts or lingering childhood whims don't reason very well, so there is inherent in life a kind of underlying anger.

Do you ever wonder why things irritate you? The weather, the traffic, the tiff with your partner, the argument with the boss, the turmoil with your child? Do you sometimes find that issues beyond your control seem to bother you? Political manipulations, foreign politics, government policies, the attitudes of sports figures, societal pressures? All of these can stir our feelings of inferiority and inadequacy and remind us of our inability to bring about the changes that we desire. Our emotional deprivation, our career failure, our aging, nurture our anger.

Can Anger Hurt You?

Mishandled anger can cause all manner of dysfunctions in the body. The greatest pleasures we experience in life can come from realistic fulfillment of our emotional drives. The greatest pain we know can come from anger gone amok. Anger that seethes beneath a calm surface can be exceedingly harmful, both mentally and physically. Turned outward, it destroys external things, including human life; herein lies the whole disturbing issue of violence in society. Turned inward, it can be similarly destructive, causing suicide or irreversible physical decline and feelings of depression.

Anger can stifle your ability to be happy. It distorts how you see things and people. It can clutter and mar the landscape of daily life. It can get in the way of your planning. Whatever your age or condition, it influences both your thoughts and your actions. Uncontrolled anger is a destructive force, whether expressed by a child wrecking a toy or an adult jeopardizing a career, a relationship, or a life.

Anger turned inward invariably causes depression. The symptoms are varied and familiar — bad disposition, poor appetite, insomnia, general malaise, irritability, feelings of hopelessness. Depression also occurs because of events that are quite real and distressing: the death of a loved one, the breakup of a marriage, the loss of something valuable, or the wrenching end of a romantic relationship. In a sense, mourning is a subtle form of anger that is being diffused and generalized. Depressed persons regard themselves as inadequate and worthless; they blame themselves for everything that is wrong; they begin to think life is not worth living.

Anger affects the body. A series of chemical adjustments mobilize for action. Sugar pours into the bloodstream to provide the needed extra energy for "fight or flight," adrenaline is secreted, the pupils of the eyes dilate. Excessive anger causes blurred vision, a defense against our rage. It all happens in a flash, and in the aftermath the heart keeps up its feverish beat, the blood pressure stays high, the chemistry is in turmoil. If there is no discharge of all this buildup, the condition is unsettling. If it becomes chronic, it can be physically harmful.

Some people, otherwise good-natured, become grouchy and not fit to live with when they get sick. Except for the hypochondriac, most of us hate being ill; we may express our anger by being excessively demanding or impatient with others. When anger persists, blood pressure remains high and we have the familiar syndrome of hypertension with its attendant dangers, a prime contributor to coronary disease.

Jeannie, a thirty-six-year-old client, gave the appearance of equanimity in spite of her problem at work. "That's the name of the game," she shrugged, "so I don't let it get to me."

When I pressed her about peer conflict and the corporate struggle for the survival of the fittest, she said she understood and accepted these pressures. But the telltale pressure, that is, her blood pressure, had for some time been at a very unhealthy 240/110 instead of the normal 120/80. The inescapable conflict in her career environment had been transferred inside, where it raged on invisibly, while outwardly she appeared poised and self-assured.

We all know of examples of calm, placid, seemingly relaxed people unaccountably suffering coronaries. We tend to think of blustery, angry types as leading contenders for coronary thrombosis. But apparently placid persons may be so guarded and circumspect that they are sitting on a powder keg of hidden rage with diseased arteries acting as a slow fuse.

Frequently, allergies, asthma, and infections are anger-related. They may be seen as an inward-directed adult form of the temper tantrum in which children hold their breath and terrify their parents. There is a strong clinical consensus that anger may be related to the most universal of afflictions: the common cold. Viruses that cause colds are around us all the time, and we host them in our bodies. Why, then, do we not have colds all the time? Normally our resistance is high enough to combat the viruses. So the question becomes not, "What causes colds?" but rather, "What lowers our resistance?"

Getting chilled, being exposed to marked temperature changes, or becoming overly fatigued can bring on a cold. But what about people who spend the whole day skiing, exhausting themselves physically in freezing weather? Could it have something to do with the fact that they are enjoying themselves and are under no emotional stress? This would lead to the conclusion that emotional stress or distress undermines our resistance. Is there a more stressful emotion than anger?

Like most bodily discomfort, a headache is a result of tension, and tension is often generated by repressed anger. When in the course of a disagreeable discussion we say to someone, "You're giving me a headache," what we more likely mean is, "You are making me angry."

Much of our pain that has emotional origins is from anger that has been turned against ourselves. When we are really intemperate, we may inflict hurt directly — kicking a table or banging our fist, sometimes even striking ourselves. More commonly the hurt is inflicted indirectly. Recently, a client confided that he just couldn't tell his wife candidly that he disliked her mother visiting them every weekend. So as not to dampen her enthusiasm, he would simply say, "Fine! It's not a problem." By the time his mother-in-law arrived, he had a splitting headache.

"I just can't stomach that person!" How familiar is this expression of anger. The gastrointestinal tract is highly sensitive to our emotional state. It is particularly prone to react to repressed rage, and it is common knowledge that gastric ulcers almost invariably involve an emotional factor. Many expressions of anger — in many languages — have to do with the lower bowel and its excretions. Colitis, the nervous affliction of the colon, is often a carry-over from childhood when the process of elimination gets much adult attention. This preoccupation with toilet training is confusing and frustrating to a small child. Surely the potential for repressed anger is there, and children who resist training and soil themselves may simply be expressing that angry confusion. As adults, of course, we cannot resort to such antisocial and infantile behavior. However, turned inward, anger can manifest itself in colitis, diarrhea, cramps, or constipation.

Are you irritated or itching to get at someone? Again, when anger is turned against ourselves it may result in a sort of attack on our own skin. The dermis is an especially fertile battlefield for our inner hostilities literally to "break out." Plagued for years by skin disorders, a client of mine in his mid-thirties had been treated by a number of dermatologists, but the symptoms continued. In three months of psychotherapy, he found considerable relief. Eventually, after he dredged up from his childhood a long litany of parental hurts and abuses against which he was helpless, a tremendous dark reservoir of repressed anger, his symptoms dissipated.

In dealing with sexual dysfunctions of any kind, I make an effort to explore the possibility of anger, overt or covert. Loss of erection or premature ejaculation may suggest repressed anger toward one's partner. Although the intention is to satisfy oneself and the sexual partner, lingering anger can surface at a most sensitive moment, resulting in disappointment for both partners. This can have a compounding effect, since the woman is not only left ungratified, but may sense in repeated episodes an intent, although consciously unintentional on the man's part, to inflict physical punishment on her. On a subconscious level, a woman may also be angry at being penetrated and may react in spite of herself by having involuntary spasms that prevent entry. This symptom is known as vaginismus. Sexual difficulties often can be traced to anger.

Often we speak of "crippling anger." Among the many causes of arthritis and its variations still under intensive research, anger turned against the self is considered by many professionals to be a contributing factor. It is believed that people who somatize anger are prime candidates for arthritic conditions. Neurologists have long been aware of the role of anger in inducing headache and backache, but there are many more complex neurological conditions — nervous tics, speech impediments such as stuttering and stammering — that point to unresolved anger as possible causes. It is not uncommon to hear that someone had a stroke in a fit of rage. It is no accident that the very term "apoplexy" has come to be a synonym for excessive and uncontrollable anger.

"He must be trying to kill himself." Did you ever hear that expression about someone acting with extreme recklessness, flooring the gas petal and cutting in front of other drivers? The acting out of anger has endless ramifications. That inner force is often very strong in the drug addict or the confirmed alcoholic. "He's drinking himself to death" is not an exaggeration. In an obese person who is "eating himself into the grave," the angry emotions may be operating more subtly, but they are there. This form of slow-motion suicide, or suicide itself, is the ultimate expression of anger turned against the self. Those who commit suicide, besides liberating themselves from their own inner turmoil, also are punishing their survivors.

If we are to understand the origins of anger, the most obvious focus of attention must be the family, for within the constellation of the family the most powerful tensions originate. When envy visited the sons of Adam and Eve, one son slew the other. Ancient and modern literature of all cultures is filled with violent acts and destructive forces — husbands and wives against each other, children against parents, parents against children, brother against brother. Homicide statistics show by overwhelming percentages that most victims knew or were related to their murderer.

It is unlikely that any of the world's evils — violence, rebellion, murder, divorce, rape, war, and massacre — could survive without the fueling energy of anger. It is, in truth, the root of all evil. And while none of us can hope to cope with all the evil around us, surely we can learn to cope more effectively with the source of the anger that lies within us. We need to understand and monitor our own angry feelings.

The good news is that anger, this most powerful emotion, if creatively channeled can be converted into strength: physical, mental, and spiritual. Five fundamental rules to consider in this regard are as follows:

First, don't let your anger control you or overwhelm you, because then you will be ineffective in healthy areas of your life. Think about the damage that it could cause to you personally as well as to others.

Second, when you sense your anger rising, be specific about why you are angry and express it directly. Instead of saying, "What's the matter with you? Are you blind or something?" say, "I'm angry that you scratched my car." Instead of asking, "Don't you ever return phone messages?" say, "I'm angry that you ignore my phone calls."

Third, if you are angry, seek socially acceptable outlets. Take a long walk, go swimming, wash your car. Do something that you have been putting off, such as cleaning your garage or cutting the grass.

Fourth, participate in sports. They are an excellent outlet for repressed anger. Tennis, racquetball, softball are great aggression venters. Anger channeled into a determination to refine your skills in a sport makes for improved performance.

Fifth, develop a hobby. Hobbies provide good ways to release anger. Finish a project you started long ago, build things, sculpt, garden, prune the trees in your backyard, paint, write; these activities often work wonders as acceptable outlets for repressed hostile feelings.

Chapter 6

DISPENSE ANGER
CONSTRUCTIVELY

Anger is a power for good or evil. It can be channeled and used not only for our mental, physical, emotional health and maturity, but also for the improvement of our intimate relationships. — MARTIN H. PADOVANI

Once we have identified the origins of anger and its destructive consequences, our next step is to explore why we are angry. Is it because we are somehow hurting? Have we been emotionally betrayed, physically injured, financially deceived or exploited? Covert or overt anger, diffused among other feelings and complicated by overlays of guilt, fear, or other emotions, is hard to define. The reasons for our anger can be elusive unless we are prepared to be thoroughly honest with ourselves and to look for hidden causes — unfulfilled wishes, inadmissible fantasies, unrealistic expectations.

Jeff, now thirty-seven and in his third relationship, looked me straight in the eye as he pounded his fist on my desk and said, "Okay, Doc, I have heard about the origins of anger, but I still feel an inner rage. Do you understand?"

Silently I nodded, affirmatively.

After several sessions I could see the results of Jeff's anger. His wounded emotions were still bleeding. When he was seven, under the threat of killing him if he told anyone of their relationship, a family friend sexually molested him. The horror was still in Jeff's dilated eyes as he described the cruel details. The molestation occurred many times, until he became very ill: he could no longer eat, lost weight, and needed to be hospitalized. Afraid and ashamed to reveal the cause of his illness — he thought nobody would believe him, and his family's friend would kill him — he kept his parents in the dark. The doctor, unable to diagnose Jeff's symptoms, prescribed medication for a spastic colon and attributed his condition to jealousy over his younger brother. "It's something Jeff will outgrow," he said.

Jeff repressed his feelings, and from the sixth grade through his early twenties, he excelled academically. A shy child by nature, at home he developed a style of compliance. But on a deeper level, the venom of anger kept poisoning his life, and as he approached thirty, he found himself in a disturbing state of depression and ambivalence. Unable to make decisions, he could not choose a viable career. The culprit, anger, surfaced and stifled many of his honest efforts to focus on some choice. Another thorny issue was his inability to let others get close. Afraid he might be rejected or hurt, he kept his relationships superficial or distant. Hesitant to give or receive love, Jeff struggled with maintaining a relationship with a woman, finding a decent job, getting along with peers, dealing with his relatives.

"Nobody understands my pain," Jeff kept repeating.

"You're right, nobody understands your pain, but you do," I said.

"But how can I stop hurting?"

"Face your anger."

"That's shrink talk," he smirked.

Facing one's angry self is not simple. There are no neat formulas or easy answers. Striving toward a reasonable accommodation with the powerful force of anger may prove to be a promising option. In the way that most medicine needs to be carefully monitored because of the harmful ingredients it contains, so as we interact with others we can observe the contents of our conversations to see how much anger they carry.

Jeff came to realize that anger wears clever disguises. In his case, the real target of his anger was himself. So when he felt tense or sad or hurt, annoyed, harassed or fed up, ready to explode, he had to ask himself: Am I angry about something? If so, what is it? Am I evading a situation? Am I afraid to face the world out there?

He was afraid. If his own parents did not understand him, he thought, how could anyone else understand him? He felt lonely and hurt. But he made himself lonely by the way he remembered his past, by the way he told stories of what had happened to him, by the way he gave up any hope that things could change.

He also evaded his situation. It was safe and predictable when he was angry. I hate my job, I don't want to go to school any more. The world stinks, I don't want any part of it. In this state of mind, he didn't have to do anything. Of course, a state of inertia and passivity nurtures a poor self-image. Our self-esteem goes down to zero. We feel worthless.

Abandoning his familiar misery for the unknown involved a risk; Jeff came to realize that even stepping out of bed every morning could cause some anxiety. But taking that calculated risk and making contact with another person opened up new horizons for healthier and productive living. He decided to stay in his current job although he didn't like it, and he returned to school to get his bachelor's degree. With some initials after his name, he stood a better chance of getting more lucrative employment. Understanding his anger did not necessarily enable him to erase his trauma or handle all the world's rage, but at least he learned how to keep his own anger from working against him.

Anger has the power to keep us miserable. We can choose to see its potential for destruction and take steps to reduce it within us. Otherwise it is the iceberg that could sink our relationship.

Here we will consider some possibilities for dealing with anger more effectively:

Acknowledge your anger. This means you learn to say to your partner, "I'm getting angry at what you're telling me." Instead of reacting and communicating your anger through a cutting remark, sarcasm, or a burst of rage, say exactly what is bothering you. It is so much easier and smoother to do this, to focus on the current issue that bothers you.

Some couples believe that being angry is wicked, and so they are ashamed or embarrassed to admit their anger to each other. It is no more difficult to say, "I'm angry," than it is to say, "I'm frightened," or "I'm hurt," or "I'm tired," or "I'm sad," or "I'm excited," or "I'm grateful," or "I'm happy." If you are to improve, maintain, or strengthen your relationship, it is important to communicate your feelings at the time they occur.

Restrain your anger. This does not mean that you do not have the right to be angry. In an appropriate situation and at an appropriate time, your feelings of anger can protect you from emotional or material damage. Anger enables you to assert yourself when and where you should. Anger can be an assertive response to antisocial behavior, to injustice, or to wrong, in order to achieve a right resolution. When angry feelings occur in a relationship, it is very important that the partners pull back and prepare themselves emotionally for handling the anger.

Challenge yourself. What is it that you want to accomplish? Do you want to punish your partner? Do you want to retaliate or get even because your feelings are hurt? Do you want to prove that you are right? Or do you want to be happy? If you want to have a happy relationship, your attitude toward your partner needs to change.

Start with this statement: "My partner is not my adversary." It does not help either of you to treat each other as enemies. What if you are angry? Then say, "I'm angry at what you said and did, but I don't want to be angry. I don't like myself in this condition. I don't want to feel distant or cold. I would rather feel close and loving." Restraining your anger prevents a rush of retaliatory anger from your partner. You may feel better if you gently invite your partner to negotiate.

Ask your partner for help. Without this step, not much progress can be made. It may require a dose of humility on your part, but once you approach your partner with a gentle spirit and make your request for help, most likely you will not be turned down. If your request for cooperation receives a positive response, your anger will be diffused and the negative feelings about your partner will evaporate. Initially you need to wait a bit and become aware of your angry feelings. Once the tide of anger subsides, focus on what made you angry. If you wish to have a loving and productive relationship, it is in your best interest, and also that of your partner, to understand what is going on and to seek viable solutions.

A Compassionate Approach

One time when it seems that there is no viable solution to angry feelings is when one of the spouses is involved in an extramarital affair. The violator of the vows may be angry because he or she perceives the other spouse as an obstacle to the affair. The fear of being discovered causes additional anger, and when the affair surfaces, the explosion is inevitable. The betrayed partner has a hard time forgiving the violator. Whatever reasons precipitate an affair, it is wise not to waste much energy blaming the other or finding excuses for it. Seek objective professional help and invest your energy in making a decision regarding what direction to take.

Regardless of the degree of your anger, it does not have to destroy your partner. Regardless of how convinced you are about your position in the relationship, you cannot change the other person by your convictions. However, you can offer an opportunity to listen with attention and care. Be fully present to your partner without any other agenda being processed on the sidelines. Pass no judgment on your partner; refrain from trying to convert him or her to your point of view, striving to be a winner.

For your own emotional recovery, examine the situation of the conflict in your relationship as calmly as you can, and then engage in a genuine dialogue with one thing in mind: to seek a mutually beneficial solution. Usually conflicts provide valuable information about who we are. A rediscovery of each other's personality helps us to understand what is truly needed to improve and strengthen the relationship. After you have learned to dispense or cope with anger effectively, you will no longer feel afraid of your own or of your partner's anger. You will feel free to be more understanding, intimate, and loving.

Life has a purpose. Take the first step to discover your purpose in the present. Your current situation may be strenuous or even painful, but so far, you are enduring it. If you stop dwelling on your past pain and future fears, your daily life may be more tolerable and even rewarding. Recalling your initial romantic love and dream of a good marriage, reconsider your present relationship. Although things may look dark and shattered, take time out to reexamine your life. Is it good for you to demolish what you have and start a new life? Is there any guarantee that you would be happier in another relationship or with another partner?

Perhaps with a more relaxed mind, you can take a compassionate look at your partner, which could be a promising start. Suppose you are unable to find anything good in your partner. Take a second, perhaps a more profound look. You may be projecting your own feelings of inadequacy. If you see your situation as hopeless, this may reflect your own state of mind at this troublesome time. If you see your partner as an angry and stubborn individual, it may be that you are angry and stubborn. If this perception is intolerable to you, then you automatically send this picture to your partner. There is a temporary relief when we blame someone else for our own conflicts.

Give yourself some credit. Once you have identified your own strengths, try to appreciate your partner's good qualities, and find joy in your efforts. Take a more positive approach and begin with what is at your fingertips. For example, say to yourself, "I'm alive. I have a mind and a functional body. I can do things that bring me satisfaction without disturbing anyone's life. I might find joy in helping others. I can make my own choices. This very moment, my choice is to make a concerted effort to employ whatever is worthwhile to save and improve my relationship."

When your partner senses your sincerity and realizes your human condition, possibly your change of heart, both of you may begin to see something good in your relationship; you may appreciate each other more, and eventually your efforts will produce results. Remember, just as you cannot coerce your partner into changing, no one can coerce you into doing anything. The choice is yours alone.

For Your Consideration

~ Appropriate anger. Allow yourself to feel it, deal with it, and be able to reveal it as a mature adult. Pouting, screaming, or throwing a temper tantrum reveals immaturity.

~ Think what the consequences would be if you were to pour out all your anger. Would you feel relieved? Perhaps. Then consider the condition of your partner, the recipient of your anger. How would he or she feel about being attacked? In any relationship, what can an angry attack really accomplish?

~ Take time out to trace the origins of your anger. Ask yourself: Can anyone really provoke as much anger as I feel right now? Does my partner have the power to ignite all this anger in me? You may be the owner of many years of deposits of anger —

painful experiences, emotional hurts, serious losses that are now surfacing.

~ If your partner has wronged you, it is only fair to define and focus on the actual wrong. Do not build up a case in order to put your partner down, punish your partner, or try to win.

~ If you flare out in anger and rage, you are not only hurting your supposed opponent, but you are hurting yourself and those around you.

~ You are not a terrible person when you admit that you have been wrong or have done wrong and your anger is an overreaction. It does not diminish your stature to apologize. Saying "I'm sorry" may pave the way for better communication.

~ If you really believe that you are right all the time, then you are only capable of a superficial emotional relationship, because you cannot risk sharing real feelings.

~ When you are faced with anger and are in front of the person to whom it is the most difficult to relate, surrender your desire to attack, overcome your inclination to respond with anger and hostility. Almost immediately you will feel better, because anger renders you weak.

~ When you suspend your angry feelings, even for a little while, the potential for a powerful relationship arises. As the clouds of anger evaporate, the warm sun shines through your body and mind. Your inner turmoil quiets down. No matter how difficult it may be, with grievances at a halt you can communicate your aggrieved feelings.

~ Even if you have good intentions and your anger never turns violent or illegal, it can prove destructive when it remains unresolved.

~ THREE ~

FORGIVE AND
FEEL FREE

If we are to gain inner peace,
we must learn to forgive each other
and let go of the anger from those who have hurt us.

⧜

Forgiveness is recognizing that we no longer need
our grudges and resentments, our hatred and self-pity.

Chapter 7

TO ERR IS HUMAN

Forgiveness is the key to inner peace. Forgiving is only for the brave — for those willing to confront their pain and accept themselves as permanently changed.

— BEVERLY FLANIGAN

One morning after breakfast, Frank Ferguson handed a little velvet box and a big card to his wife. "Happy Anniversary!" he said with charm as he kissed her.

"For me?" she asked with genuine surprise and gave him a hug and a kiss. Gently she opened the card and read, "You're everything to me. You're someone I can count on, someone I love with all my heart. For the last twenty years I've enjoyed being with you. I've always loved you. I want to tell you how happy I am, and I'm especially thankful today on our twentieth anniversary."

"I love you, too," Annette said with feelings of gratitude. "At times I have been hard on him, wanting him to satisfy my own needs," she thought. "It's nice to know that he still loves me so much."

The Fergusons had a good married relationship, and they both felt that their two daughters, one in college and the other a senior in high school, were a blessing. They owned a beautiful house, he had a good job, and she worked out of her office at home doing consulting work which brought in a handsome income.

Hardly able to stem tears of joy, Annette opened the box. "Oh, my God," she screamed, "a diamond bracelet! You must have spent a fortune!"

"You're worth it," he said, hurrying out of the front door.

"Not even a goodbye kiss?"

"I'll be late for work," he shouted as he pulled his car out of the driveway.

Annette sat in the kitchen drinking another cup of coffee. She could not take her eyes off the diamond bracelet. One by one she counted the little rocks — twenty, one for each year of their married life. She pondered the good times and the bad times they had shared together.

Annette took her mother shopping that day, and she returned home early enough to prepare an elaborate anniversary dinner with champagne, music, and candlelight. She put on a sexy dress that Frank had bought for her fortieth birthday the previous month, fastened the bracelet on her wrist, and waited for her husband's arrival. It was to be a long wait. Frank did not return.

It was one of those strange cases we read about and find incredible. He moved out of state, leaving no forwarding address, no goodbye message, not a note, not a phone call. Three days later, Annette received a registered letter from a lawyer, stating that her husband had filed for divorce and that she should retain a lawyer to represent her. When her daughters found out, they could not believe that their dad would do such a terrible thing. "I thought you guys really and truly loved each other," wrote her daughter from college.

Annette's world fell apart. A commitment she thought they had made for life was shredded in a moment without a warning. "There must be another woman in his life, and I was too dumb to suspect it," she thought. She threw the bracelet on her dresser. "It's hard to believe that all these years he has been deceiving me." Feeling unforgivably wounded and sensing the full force of her injury, she kept repeating, "How dare he? I have never done anything to hurt him. He never complained about our marriage."

"Forgive? How could I possibly forgive him?" Annette Ferguson told me tearfully. "He never gave me a sign that he was unhappy. I thought we had a very good marriage."

Lawyers represented both spouses at court, properties were divided equally, and reasonable alimony was granted to Annette. There was no further contact between Frank and Annette until several years later when their younger daughter was graduating from college. As their eyes finally met during the ceremony, Annette felt her heart filling with an eerie and uncontrollable rage.

To prevent herself from public embarrassment, she rushed to the rest room and burst into tears. When she saw the reflection of her swollen eyes in the mirror, she realized that her wounded heart needed healing. "Will I ever be able to forgive my husband?" she wondered.

Without much concern, Frank Ferguson was able to sever his most intimate relationship and leave behind his closest companion. We can hardly imagine his wife's pain and sorrow, her rage and humiliation. It was not just abandonment but also the destruction of everything she had believed in: their life together, their dreams of the future, their daughters, and even the validity of the history they had shared. Not only was she robbed of companionship and love but also of the future she had anticipated, a future that crumbled overnight because her husband had changed his direction.

Annette wallowed in pain for a long time. Unable to *let go* of the injury her husband had caused her, she felt embittered. Her need for revenge, for righting the wrong, for undoing the hurt gave her no peace.

Forgiveness makes it possible to release negative emotions that result from a painful experience. When Frank Ferguson walked away from his wife, this hurtful action became part of the dead past. It was up to Annette to make a choice: to use all her strength to forgive and let go of the hurt, or to hold on to the anger and hatred. She chose the latter, and consequently she continued to suffer.

In her therapy, Annette realized that holding on to the hurtful relationship with her husband prevented her from doing anything worthwhile for herself. She became passive and bored with her life, and instead of connecting with healthy people to seek solace, she resorted to isolation and indifference. To quiet her pain, she ate frequently, and drank wine. She had never smoked in her life, but now she found nicotine to be relaxing. Any one person who is unable to forgive suffers emotionally and physically. Wounded emotions eventually affect the body. When Annette went to the doctor for a complete physical, the doctor discovered that she had a growth in her left breast; the biopsy indicated that it was cancerous and needed to be removed. Eventually she had a mastectomy. Could her emotional hurt have contributed to her cancer?

If hurt is part of life — and at one time or another we all get hurt — we need to find a way to heal. Otherwise, unhealed hurts linger on, damaging our existence and causing more pain. Think of a wrong done to you as a snake bite. There are two sources of pain. One is the bite itself, the visible wound, which cannot be undone. It's there, it bleeds or hurts, and you can see the wound where the fangs penetrated the flesh. The second source of pain is the venom that circulates in your blood. This is the killer. No one has ever died from a snake bite; it is the aftermath of the venom permeating the body that can be fatal. A similar situation occurs with hatred and the desire to seek revenge. Although the wound has externally healed, the unforgiving attitude continues to poison your inner world. Only you have the power to extract the killer poison of unforgiveness.

Like love and acceptance, forgiveness is one of the most important ingredients in a relationship. You have heard the saying, "To err is human, to forgive, divine." Nothing could be more powerful in our relationships than the realization that as imperfect humans we all make mistakes. A relationship consists of two humans; neither is an angel. In addition to our unwitting errors, we knowingly and often without legitimate reason cause one another to suffer. We lie, break promises, humiliate each other, use abusive or violent language, neglect or ignore each other, betray each other, pummel and abandon each other. We often do these things not to our enemies but to the people closest to us, precipitating serious pain in intimate relationships. Emotional injuries are often left festering and unresolved, causing not only ill feelings but physical ailments.

Think back to the last time someone really hurt you or wronged you or took something that belonged to you, whether it was a possession or an opportunity. Did you not feel like retaliating? Did you not feel like fighting for your *rights?* This is a normal reaction to being taken advantage of or being hurt. Think what your reaction does to you, both on the emotional and the physical levels. Improper response to your injury automatically impairs your own health. We have no joy or peace when others have injured us in some way. We want to strike back, get revenge, or get even. Rarely do we consider responding gently to individuals who hurt us, and rarely do we seek reconciliation. Pain and anger prevent us from being understanding, patient, or kind to people who have wronged us. Our anger filters into other relationships that otherwise could be rewarding. People sense that something is wrong with us and either avoid us or maintain a distance from us. As a result, we feel alienated, confused, disturbed, embittered, and passive, and we do not really know how to regain peace.

Have you ever been hurt? Were you abused as a child? Sexually molested? Did you feel neglected or rejected by your parents? Did one or both of your parents favor a certain sibling over you? Did you suffer through your parents' marriage or divorce as a child? Were you coerced into pursuing a different career from the one that you wanted? Did the partner of your dreams betray you for the love of another?

If you answer yes to any of these questions, you may be on the brink of being set free from a suffocating bondage that you did not know was keeping you a victim. What happened in your past can make you sick if you treat your hurts as precious artifacts that must be displayed in your living room. We do not have to be victims, because we can invite into our lives what has always been the only remedy for healing broken hearts and damaged emotions.

We need to practice the art of forgiveness. Most of the wounds that we experience are not unforgivable. We can put them behind us and go on with our lives. We must learn to forgive each other and let go of those who have hurt us if we are to regain inner peace.

If you have been betrayed by your partner, if you have been abused, forgiveness can set you free from the hurtful experience. If you do not choose to forgive the one who hurt you, then you will continue to suffer from the destructive emotional energy you have created, in spite of the fact that what started the process was the act of the victimizer. If you choose to let go of the feelings of revenge and anger and replace them with forgiveness, then you free yourself from the negative cycle of energy.

Forgiveness is not forgetting. It is not condoning or justifying or explaining why persons acted toward you as they did. Forgiveness is not absolution. When you forgive persons who hurt you, it does not mean the offenders are off the hook. The offenders are still responsible for their crime, and they must make their own peace. Forgiveness is not a form of self-sacrifice, of swallowing your true feelings and playing the martyr.

Forgiveness takes time and happens naturally as a result of confronting painful past experiences and finally allowing old wounds to heal. Forgiveness occurs when we become aware that it is a gift of the heart inherent in every person.

A Desire for Healing

Forgiveness is a by-product of an ongoing healing process. It is a feeling of wellness and freedom and acceptance. We find it waiting for us when we reach a point where we stop expecting the offenders to pay for their offense or make it up to us in some way. Forgiveness is recognizing that we no longer need our grudges and resentments, our hatred and self-pity. We do not need them as an excuse for getting less out of life than we want or deserve. Forgiveness is moving on. It is freeing up and putting to better use the energy once consumed by holding grudges and harboring resentments. It is recognizing that we have better things to do with our lives and then doing them.

You may be waiting for the day when your partner comes to you on bended knee, apologizing profusely and begging your forgiveness. If that day ever comes, the apology would not be enough. It would not relieve your pain or evaporate your rage. It would not change your life or make you happier, healthier, or more at peace with yourself. You are the only one who can do that as you let go and let your inner self be your source of unconditional forgiveness.

Lennie and Nancy had three children, an eight-year-old girl and two teenage sons. After seventeen years of marriage, Lennie and Nancy separated for three years. Neither of them went to a lawyer to terminate the marriage officially. Nancy initially fell in love with her boss, who supposedly had a bad marriage and planned to divorce his wife. The affair and the promises made by her boss pulled Nancy out of her family. Eventually, her boss returned to his wife, and Nancy, brokenhearted, lived alone; she felt too guilty to return to her husband and children, although her priest and her parents advised her to go back. Confused and guilty, she entered into another relationship and moved in with a divorced man. Her hopes were high because she loved him and expected to marry him. She lived with him for two years, and then one day a phone call from his ex-wife upset her life. The ex-wife explained that she had reconciled with her former husband, and they planned to remarry.

When Nancy confronted her lover, he admitted that he had made up his mind to return to his ex-wife.

Lennie, in spite of his circumstances — having to take care of his motherless children and his home — remained faithful to his convictions. He did not believe in divorce and kept hoping that his wife would return some day. Although he perceived his wife to be an unhappy and confused person, he never said a bad word about her to his children. As for his deeper feelings of frustration, he sought psychotherapy to sustain himself emotionally and to enable himself to direct the growth of his children.

Nancy lived in a one-room apartment with no friends and no direction in her life. She worked hard to pay her bills, and periodically she bought presents for her children. The boys, one now a junior and the other a senior in high school, missed their mother and wanted her back. The girl did not want to see her mother and emphatically said, "Daddy, I don't want her back. I'll take care of you. We don't need her."

Lennie had his own feelings of anger and real contempt for his wife's betrayal and for the shame she had brought upon his household. When he saw his wife conversing with their older son, however, he had an instant recollection of the boy's birth and the excitement he and Nancy had experienced when they brought the baby home. Suddenly, he felt touched and wished things were different, but the wound was very deep. "It's too late," he said to himself. "Even if she wants to come back, I don't think I want her. I have no feelings for her."

Lennie was hurting, and during his therapy he came to the realization that if he were to function as a responsible father to his children and a responsible citizen to himself and his environment, he had to do something about his inner fragmentation. He needed to heal.

According to Elisabeth Kübler-Ross, people pass through five stages in reconciling themselves to death: denial, anger, bargaining, depression, and acceptance. Partners who suffer a break in their relationship go though similar stages in order to reconcile themselves to the death of the relationship and to the resurrection of a new self.

In the denial stage, Lennie reacted in shock: "No, not me. I haven't done anything wrong to her. I've been a loving and caring husband and a good provider for my family. How could she leave me? There must be something wrong." This stage leads naturally to the next stage.

In the anger stage, "Why me?" became the cry. Abandoned and left behind with the children, hurting, he resented the fact that other couples seemed happy together, while his marriage had fallen apart.

When the anger subsided, Lennie entered the bargaining stage: "Maybe I can apologize. I can change and be a better husband if only she will give me a chance. Maybe I didn't give her enough attention." He comforted himself by saying, "I still love her; she is everything to me. If she comes back, we can work things out." This sort of claim is a prelude to the next stage, depression.

Depression is the "Yes, me" stage. Lennie began to realize that his wife was not coming back. Having spent his time brooding over the rights and wrongs of their relationship, he gradually alienated himself from people and withdrew from his friends. Cigarettes, food, and wine became his companions. He gave the impression that he needed nobody, but inside, his stomach churned daily. He became passionately involved with his children and made sure they lacked nothing.

Lennie eventually entered the final stage, acceptance, when he was able to say, "My marriage is over. This is as far as it was meant to go. There is nothing that I can do but accept my reality." This is not a happy stage, but neither is it unhappy. It is not resignation from life; it is really a victory of transformation. When he gradually chose to see his situation as real, he was able to let go of her and his life with her and pursue his personal healing.

If you are currently suffering from some serious hurt, it may be difficult for you to understand the deeper meaning of forgiveness. What actually goes on in your mind and wounded heart, the inner turmoil that you are suffering because of the person that has injured you, no one can fathom except you. Forgiving that person may be at the bottom of your priority list.

Let me clarify: The true meaning of the verb "forgive" is "let go." In essence, it is only God who forgives. We humans are able to only "let go," and that's the best we can expect. If you "let go," it does not mean that you resign from life and living. It means that the outcome is no longer in your hands. If you "let go" of the hurt, it does not mean that you deny reality around you. It means you have no choice but to accept the pain as real and allow healing to take over.

Forgiveness is a process that can be painful, and at times it seems unending. Whatever your pain, whatever your situation, you cannot afford to hold on for one more day to an unforgiving spirit. Forgiveness is not a force to be used. For example, you cannot say, "Oh, I've forgiven her — it's all behind me," as you experience a sense of superiority. Forgiveness, like a fragrance, needs to be inhaled and cherished. You must get sincerely involved in the process of forgiving the person who has hurt you. Let go of ·the hurt so that you may heal and find out what it means to be free and emotionally healthy.

The abundance of literature on forgiveness describes the process as a concerted transaction that takes place between two parties — the offended person and the offender. But for a transaction to occur, both people must be present to participate and both must be willing to do so. However, for many people who have been hurt by those they have loved, this is simply not the situation. Most people forgive alone, with little or no help from others. Like any major achievement in your life, forgiveness takes patience and faith that the process will produce the desired results: your personal healing and peace of mind.

The following steps may be of help:

Step One. Reevaluate your emotional injury and the subsequent pain. Reassess the nature of right and wrong that occurred between you and the person who harmed you. If it takes two to make or break a relationship, determine honestly your responsibility. How much control can you have over your injury? *Almost none.* You do have control over your life. As you explore the damage done, your perceptions about justice, trust, and betrayal may be enhanced. No matter how much pain you are experiencing right now, you can still connect with some healthy people who can help you interpret the events of your life and give them meaning.

Step Two. Admit your pain. Say to yourself, "This is my pain — no one else's. Other people may have been hurt, too, but I can't do anything about that. I must forgive, let go of this injury, because this is the one that maintains my pain." Separate your injuries from those of other people. Do not compare or identify your situation with anybody else's. Many people suffer from toothaches, and you may empathize with them, but do you really feel their pain? However, when your tooth hurts, you truly feel that pain. Accept your pain as an uninvited guest, and keep it in perspective.

Step Three. Someone is accountable for causing you such emotional damage. Once you identify the offender, you may put all the blame on that person or ceaselessly ask, "Why did this happen to me?" Although the question is normal, you may never be satisfied with the answer. Those who have hurt you will seek to defend themselves or give you unsatisfactory reasons. It is better to employ the services of a reliable person, a lawyer or mediator, to responsibly pursue your rights. Disciplining or punishing the offender is a matter of law and order. Your part is to pull your inner resources together and eventually to let go.

Step Four. If you have tried all possible methods to let go of your injury and you still feel the pangs of anger, rest assured that no rage or punishment on your part will restore your inner peace. There is nothing left but to move forward to the final action of forgiving. Are you ready? It takes great strength to be able to forgive. Forgiveness emerges from the inner self, and it is reinforced by the good qualities that a person possesses — compassion, self-esteem, self-respect. As a forgiver, you may seek out people who feel as you do about forgiveness, new friends who can be understanding and supportive.

Step Five. The choice to forgive is yours. This implies that you let go of the other person's offense. It does not mean that the other person was right and you were wrong; it only means that even though you are hurt, you have no expectation of the offender. Choosing to forgive increases self-esteem and personal responsibility. In essence, what you are saying is this: The person who hurt me is no longer responsible for the way my life will evolve. I am responsible.

Chapter 8

THE POTENTIAL
OF PERSISTENCE

Everything is possible to a person who believes.
— MARK 9:23

During this writing, Lennie came to see me. He looked a bit different, a new person, a changed man. There was a glow of joy about his appearance, a tone of confidence in his voice.

I meant to call you," he said. "Nancy and I have started marriage counseling with her therapist."

"How does it look to you?" I asked, withholding my surprise. "Their marriage died a long time ago," I thought.

"Well, Nancy telephoned me one day and told me that she had started counseling with a woman therapist whom she liked. Then she asked me if I would join her for a few sessions. I saw no harm in the idea so I agreed to go."

"It sounds to me as if you're both giving your relationship another chance," I said.

"Nancy has found comfort and peace with this woman, and her total attitude about life seems to have changed."

"Lennie, I know your feelings about Nancy. I'm happy for you. When you believe in something, it can happen."

"I want to come back and see you a few more times. I need to have my thoughts checked. Nancy might join us."

When Lennie returned to my office, he appeared to have some doubts; he wondered if he was doing the right thing, attempting a reconciliation with his wife. He told me how remorseful Nancy felt and how willing she was to restore her marriage.

It was evident that, along with his doubts, Lennie had strong feelings about his family. He wanted his wife back; he had thought about her every day since she had abandoned the household. He loved her and, to my knowledge, had no desire to start a relationship with another woman.

"To make an end is to make a beginning," T. S. Eliot claimed.

"A new beginning! We must learn to live each day each hour, yes, each minute as a new beginning, as a unique opportunity to make everything new," Henri J. M. Nouwen advised. Both Lennie and Nancy had to deal with the ending of a life that was troublesome. To make a genuine beginning was not as simple as moving back together again and letting bygones be bygones, however. It was important to do more than simply persevere.

They needed an inner realignment, an emotional restoration. In order to launch into a new beginning, both had to let go of past wrongs and forgive themselves for the hurts they had caused each other. Did they take a chance in getting back together? Yes. Life offered a challenge. They took it.

With amazement I observed their growth and transition move in a more mature direction. In spite of initial anxieties and confusions that arose, they put away old styles and dysfunctional ways of interacting, and they discovered who each really was. They were both vulnerable and agreed to be gentle with each other. When hurtful memories surfaced, they treated them with compassion and without judgment. They made a conscious effort to avoid remarks such as: "Why did you do such a stupid thing?" "I can't believe what you did to me!" "You should know better than that. I told you so." Instead, they began to use affirmations with a sprinkling of praise: "I'm proud of you. I do like the way you do things. You're a good helper. You have so much to give. I appreciate your presence in my life."

As they both focused more on the positive and spoke the language of the heart, they resumed a practice they had followed in their early years of marriage. Every day they gave each other a gentle hug. Periodically, the hug became a little romantic exchange.

In time, each felt responsible for the other's well-being. They made a decision that some quality time together was a priority. For example, Lennie reduced the number of hours that he spent on the Internet and took an interest in domestic life; Nancy reduced her excessive involvement with her mother and began to show more interest in her husband's job.

They both said yes to their marriage and proceeded to establish some goals. As they focused on making their marriage better, Nancy and Lennie also pursued personal projects.

Nancy had always wanted to be an interior decorator, but she had felt hindered by obligations to her family, a daughter and two sons still at home. She realized that the path to follow had been there all the time. She had the desire, the aesthetic eye and talent, but she had not seriously considered her inner yearnings. The obstacle had not been her family, but her own doubts about her abilities. Her husband wanted her to be a happy woman and pursue her dream. He offered to help in every way he could. When she began to take courses in college, she felt happier and her home life no longer appeared to be an obstacle.

Lennie, whose office job provided little opportunity for physical activity, joined the YMCA and began to exercise regularly. After a good workout, he came home with more energy and in a better frame of mind. One of his dreams was to write poetry, so he subscribed to a magazine for poets and writers. Late in the evenings when everyone was in bed, he spent an hour at his word processor composing poems; he shared his compositions with Nancy.

When Lennie came home from work tired and discouraged, Nancy would say a few comforting words and give him a sympathetic hug; he found her reception helped to dispel his stress. It was helpful for Nancy to share with her husband some of her ideas about interior decorating. When they shared hurts, disappointments, and difficulties, they were careful not to burden each other emotionally.

When partners gain a sense of fulfillment from other sources, they feel more secure, independent, and strong. They don't make unrealistic demands on their marriage. They accept life's pain, its loneliness, and its stress as something they must handle — when the chips are down — themselves. Life can be more pleasant if we don't indulge in wallowing in sad news and tragic events. Some of the stresses of life can be shared with a friend or someone who is receptive and willing to discuss the ills of society. If you have a personal or a family issue to discuss with your partner, do not avoid it by discussing the tragedies of the world. Find the appropriate time when you and your partner are emotionally available to each other and bring up the subject.

Nancy and Lennie, monitored by their therapist, maintained a healthy balance with each other. What at one time seemed an irreparable situation, now became a challenge. They wanted their marriage to work, and they diligently tried to do what it takes to make a marriage work. Above all, letting go of the crisis they both painfully experienced brought about a transformation, individually and as a married couple. It became a new relationship in which both felt strong.

With a personal awareness of their needs and a realistic outlook on life and living, they evolved into an admirable couple. Dreams, myths, and expectations, as creative as they had been, were placed in perspective as they moved on with immediate day-to-day tasks. Lennie accepted a new position in a different company, and Nancy found a corner of their house where she set up an office to accommodate her freelance career in interior decorating. Meanwhile, they changed residence, made some new friends, and began to see life as a rewarding experience. Although their life had changed dramatically and nothing could ever be the same, this time around being together appeared promising.

Forgive Yourself

As we learn and practice the art of forgiveness, we must learn to forgive ourselves. When you are able to apply patiently the five steps discussed above, you will undoubtedly feel relief. Feeling better is a result of your decision to forgive, to let go of the emotional injury. "I have tried one by one all those steps," you might say, "but still I don't feel any relief." That may be true when you are at the initial stages of letting go. The pain or the memory of the hurt is still lurking in your heart. The emotional scar is still there. However, when you have forgiven your offender, you have accomplished a major achievement. To reinforce your ability to forgive, you need to take one more step, a most important one: forgive yourself.

Have you ever said, "Am I stupid? How could I have ever done such a thing?" Or, "I can't believe I was conned into such an insidious situation." Statements of this nature imply an indirect desire to punish yourself. On the surface, you may say, "I've come to terms with things. I'm only human. I made a mistake." Or,

"Well, God forgives." But on a deeper level, you feel bad; you may have a need to punish yourself, and so you resort to self-accusations. Actually what you are saying is, "I feel worthless. Anyone else may deserve to be forgiven, but not me. I'm really not a good person."

Self-forgiveness does not mean condoning what you have done or absolving yourself of the responsibilities and consequences of your actions; rather it emphasizes them. Self-forgiveness provides room for self-exploration, accountability, self-acceptance, and change. With all our limitations, we accept who we are and move on to improve our attitude and perform better; possibly we can right the wrongs — if wrongs can be realistically righted — and refine our style of life. If you are disappointed with yourself because of the way you have lived your life or the way you have treated someone or the way you have reacted to a certain issue, then you may find self-forgiveness unattainable. As a result, you allow self-condemnation or self-pity or self-punishment to block the healing and happiness that you deserve as a human being.

What happens when we persist in not forgiving ourselves? Think for a moment how you feel when you say, "I'm unforgivable; I'm a failure." You build up reserves of guilt, you become passive and emotionally numb, and you are controlled by a worthless, joyless feeling.

As I bring this chapter to a close, I hear soft radio music coming from the adjacent room. Suddenly, the music is interrupted by the announcement of tragic news. A young man, nineteen years old, shot himself and died in the back yard of his home. The shocking point of this tragedy is that it was his view of himself that caused the sad ending. Apart from the ultimate pain, his parents had to live with the burden of his handwritten farewell note, which included the sentence: "I'm a failure." Could he have failed all nineteen years of his life? Unfortunately, that is how he saw himself as he pulled the trigger. We will never know what sort of conflicts existed within his tormented soul. We can only speculate that, had he been guided to forgive and accept himself, things would have been different. In our darkest moments, there is a ray of hope as we accept our human condition and learn to forgive ourselves.

The source of many inner conflicts is the refusal to forgive self.

People suffering emotional conflicts need to forgive themselves before they can heal and regain peace. Simply stated, we will not be
able to forgive our partners, our brothers and sisters, our parents,
or anyone else unless we learn to forgive ourselves. It may be difficult to forgive ourselves; we have to work at it, but it can be done.
It may be a challenge but it is also the key to our mental stability,
our emotional and spiritual health, and our healing.

Judging yourself severely will distance you from significant
people in your life or a promising future. It will inhibit your own
potential, and the only way to escape is to forgive yourself. If un-
acknowledged anger or guilt stands in your way, I invite you to be
gentler to yourself and move forward with courage toward a new
beginning. Self-forgiveness will almost immediately show you that
you can have a better life.

Take an inventory of your beliefs and ask yourself how well
they serve you in living a life of harmony and purpose. If your
belief system violates irrevocable rules and hurts others, it is time
to change it. No angry reaction, no guilt, no self-flagellation over
things that you consider mistakes is going to provide any peace.
Look at the lessons that your mistakes have taught you. Truly,
success provides joy, but only for a while, but a mistake hurts and
lingers on, a reminder and a lasting lesson.

Judging your action as wrong may cause you a tinge of guilt;
this is appropriate and may prevent its recurrence. Your ability
to evaluate and respond to wrongs that you may have committed
will pave the way to self-forgiveness. As much as you may need to
be forgiven by a significant other, it is imperative that you forgive
yourself. This becomes easier when you accept who you really are,
an imperfect human being with many good qualities and some bad
ones. Self-acceptance will turn into self-respect, and when you are
filled with self-respect, then you will be able to respect others.

Once you learn to release your judgment of another person,
you are actually releasing judgment of yourself. When you stop
scrutinizing or judging others, you have already started to forgive
yourself for whatever negative aspects of yourself you see in them.
Your willingness to forgive yourself is the necessary step to being in
harmony with your partner, and, above all, to experiencing inner
harmony. This inner harmony will fill your heart with love and
give you permission to have the life of your choice.

For Your Consideration

~ When you were younger, your mistakes were your most useful tool. What you do right today is because of what you learned from yesterday's mistakes.

~ If yesterday's mistakes left you with a deposit of guilt, you have lost an effective tool for growth. Guilt guarantees passivity and a search for punishment.

~ If you consider yourself a failure, the word "failure" is itself a judgment, and if you label yourself a failure in any context, you are wasting precious time in judging rather than accepting yourself.

~ To restore and maintain good emotional and physical health, entertain positive thoughts about yourself.

~ We have choices. Our state of happiness or unhappiness is a result of our choice about life and living. The choices that we make condition our lives. When we choose to forgive ourselves, we set our mind to offer forgiveness to others.

Chapter 9

EVENTS DON'T CHANGE

*Two roads diverged in a wood, and I —
I took the one less traveled by,
And that has made all the difference.*

— ROBERT FROST

The simple wisdom in Robert Frost's "The Road Not Taken" is a note of relief to those of us who would like to make decisions openly, painlessly, clearly, confidently, and joyfully. But life is not that simple. Every day we make choices, and then unanticipated events occur. How we react to these events and what road we choose to take — these are what shape and form our life.

Certain events that occur in a relationship can cause a great deal of pain. They can even destroy the relationship. Can we really change something that has already happened? Our minds are not chalkboards that we can easily erase. Memory registers events, especially painful ones. How we interpret these events can be the source of seething pain or lingering hostile feelings.

Sandy sat in my office three feet away from her husband, Gary. Although she was a beautiful brunette, slightly on the heavy side, her forty-one-year-old face was ugly with fury as she laced into him with accusations at the top of her shrill voice, "The marriage is over. I'll never forgive you. You deceived me."

After thirty-five minutes of detailed description of the wrongs in their relationship, I managed to elicit some basic information. They had been married for nineteen years — "terrible years," according to Sandy — and they had two teenage boys, "spoiled brats." It seemed to me that this marriage was breathing its last. The previous week, Sandy had found out that Gary had been carrying on an affair for six months. For some time she had suspected that something strange was going on, but she had said to herself, "Not my Gary. He's too devoted to his family. Besides, he's a workaholic, in love with his work as an advertising agent."

"When was the last time you made love?"

They looked at each other resentfully, and then turned to me with an "are-you-for-real" sneer. Sandy said, "Last night. Why?"

Puzzled by the answer, I pondered how these two could make love in an atmosphere reeking of hostility. I learned that a week before Sandy, while searching through Gary's pockets, found a love letter from the "other woman." She put Gary through the holy inquisition. She bombarded him with vulgar questions, soliciting specific information and details. She ripped into him with manic fury, throwing things, punching him, and spitting in his face. For an entire week, their house was a battlefield. The children felt fearful and confused.

"What happened last night?" I asked.

Gary looked contrite, but Sandy volunteered the answer. "I'm stupid. He fell on his knees and cried, and I gave in — that was my mistake. I thought I could forgive him, but I don't think I can trust him anymore." She cried. "This is the end, and I know in my heart that no marriage counselor — I don't mean to put your profession down — but no one can persuade me to change my mind. I can't take him back."

"Sorry, Sandy," Gary interrupted. "I did a terrible thing to our marriage. But I learned something."

"Sure, you learned one thing — that I'm stupid."

"No, I learned that I love you more than anything else in the world."

"And you committed adultery to prove it. Get it into your head, Gary. It's over. I don't want you near me or near the children. I've spoken to my lawyer."

When an affair takes place, regardless of who the culprit is, I search into the labyrinth of the relationship to discover the reason why the man or the woman went off the track. To pursue the metaphor, why would a train derail if the tracks are frequently checked and are inviolate? Something goes wrong somewhere along the line as couples interact, and one of them, and at times both, are derailed and look outside their relationship to find fulfillment. Why?

Many are the precursors of an affair, but as I sat on the edge of my chair and momentarily thought of these two making love the previous night, I leaned forward toward them and said, "Sandy and Gary, I'm not a miracle worker, but I think I can help you."

"Thanks, but no thanks," Sandy said.

"Give me a chance, please. Maybe the doctor can help us," said Gary.

"Sandy, I know you love this man with all your heart, but right now you're hurting a lot. I also know that you did not come here this evening to defend your case or accuse and punish Gary. I think you came here because you value your marriage vows."

She nodded skeptically as she opened her pocketbook and pulled out her checkbook. "Pay me next time, when you come back," I said, taking a hopeful risk.

"You're a sneaky shrink, aren't you?" she said, shaking her head and simulating a smile.

"Sneaky? No, Sandy, but I care especially for people who hurt a lot."

"When can you see us again?" she asked.

Before I saw both partners again, I made appointments to see each one separately. I wanted to learn details about each spouse and find out the degree of their emotional involvement with each other. Personally, I operate on the premise of hope and on a personal conviction that under the pain we experience lies the potential for healing and the quest for love.

Sandy came back the following week, eager to tell me about the other woman and how she discovered her husband's affair. It was important for her to tell me how she had become suspicious and had hired a detective to prove to herself that there was another woman. When she found out the truth, she no longer wanted any part of Gary. A few minutes after her fury had subsided, a tear escaped her eyes and she smiled. "Maybe someday I'll be able to find someone who can love me and have respect for me."

"I'm sure there must be somebody out there," I said and remained silent for a few seconds to let Sandy's soul regain some serenity.

"Well, aren't you going to suggest something?"

"I could suggest something to provide healing for you, but I'm not sure if that's what you want me to do. You're still very angry."

"You know I hurt?"

I nodded a silent yes.

"What am I going to do about him?"

"Him?"

"Yes, my husband, the rat."

"Directing your anger at Gary is like investing money in a losing stock."

"You mean I shouldn't be angry?"

"Anger is energy, but you need to appropriate it wisely. What I mean is that anger is not going to resolve your situation."

"But I can't help feeling angry."

"Do you want to save your marriage?"

Sandy did not answer. She rested her head on the palm of her hand and thought. "I guess I want the marriage, but my feelings for Gary are shattered. Because of the way I feel, I don't want him to touch me."

"You may have a hard time accepting what I'm about to tell you. But if you truly want your marriage, the repair that's needed may have to start with you."

"With me?" She raised her voice and her face turned red. "Why me? Is it my fault? He messed up."

"I know that, and he may have to clean up his mess, but because you want to save the marriage, I propose that we start with you."

She nodded, not totally convinced.

"I believe in the art of the possible," I continued, "and, until I see you again, I would like you to consider and practice the following points:

1. Do know that I am on your side. As a marriage therapist, I'm never in favor of breaking up families. I would like to see healing and restoration between you and Gary. If you both agree to reconcile, I will need your cooperation.

2. Don't jump to conclusions. While your situation seems hopeless at the moment, if you handle it with care, it may prove to be an opportunity for open and meaningful communication. It's time to see the meaning of the affair. Stop dealing with its wrongness, observe your feelings, and listen to your husband's thoughts. Maybe you have failed to meet some of his needs.

3. Listen but try not to react. He may claim that you never really loved him or that he never really loved you. Don't jump to the defensive. He might be trying to convince himself that since he did not feel fulfilled at home, he found fulfillment with another woman. On a deeper level, he probably does not believe this to be true, but now, between shame and guilt, he struggles to justify the affair. Don't antagonize him.

4. Do not mention the other woman again. Whoever she is, try to eliminate her from your mind as if she were a malignant tumor that must be removed; otherwise, the affair will cause the death of the relationship. It may be difficult for you to forget or ignore this other woman, but right now, it's imperative that you do. Besides, a romance or real love may have developed between her and your husband. Whatever it means, don't become a part of it by verbally attacking her. Try to put her out of your mind for at least one week.

5. Do not wage war against the other woman. You don't need to see her or talk to her or call her relatives about the affair. Anything negative that you might say against her, any angry threats, justified as you may be, make you undesirable. Your husband, either verbally or mentally, will jump to her defense. Angry tactics may push him a step closer to her, and thus exclude reconciliation with you.

6. Do not call or visit a lawyer. If you have already called a lawyer, I suggest that you call back and say that you are not ready for divorce proceedings. Some lawyers can show a great deal of empathy for a hurting woman. They may listen attentively as the computer registers the time you spend with them, and they will build up a case to support your angered self. Then divorce proceedings will be processed, and your bill will skyrocket.

7. Tell Gary that you love him. I know you don't feel like it, because you're still angry. Telling him that no matter what, you are willing to give the relationship a chance because you care. He probably feels that you don't love him. If you continue to point your finger at him, reminding him that he

committed adultery, you will never win. You might as well close this book."

We Do Have Choices

Like Sandy, you may think that following the above suggestions is too much to expect of a person who has been wronged. I understand with you. However, what we need to consider is that in any relationship, success or failure depends on how two people interact and what qualities they contribute to their relationship. Sandy and Gary's situation reflects the choices that they made during the years of their marriage. As we shall see later on, both contributed to the break. If a restoration is desired, each has to acknowledge individually what he/she contributed to cause the deterioration of the relationship.

Alone in another session, Sandy admitted that she took Gary for granted. In her words: "Handsome, with a sharp sense of humor, motivated, hard-working, generous, from a good family, he loved me, and he was kind to my parents. I felt blessed having everything a woman could want in life. We traveled, we took vacations in choice places, we entertained friends, we created a warm atmosphere in our home. On the whole, we were happy. Love-making was a delight, and we were both sensitive about pleasing each other. When children arrived, I sensed that Gary began to drift away from me. He did work harder, I admit, and he stayed very late at the office. When I pointed out that it was important for me to have him around to extend a helping hand with the kids, he said, 'Let's get a nanny.' "

" 'I guess, he doesn't want to be bothered,' I thought.

"During the period of child bearing and caring, there was so much to be done that I didn't have much time for Gary. In the evenings when he came home, I was exhausted from being involved with the children all day. I wanted him to take over and give them baths and put them to bed, but his response was, 'I'm too tired.' I was tired too. I felt alone and lonely. Our love-making declined, and feeling consumed with the children's welfare, I was emotionally and physically unavailable to him and disappointed with my marriage. Even our house began to look untidy. I got to the point where all I cared about was the health and well-being of my children, nothing else. Meanwhile, I gained a great deal of weight, which I thought I would lose once the children were at a more manageable age. I began to do some exercises. I've lost about twenty pounds, but I still have a way to go."

"Did Gary ever verbalize his feelings about the changes that were occurring in your married life?" I asked.

"He did say that I should watch my weight. I got angry at him. 'What do you expect after two pregnancies?' I said. 'It's hard for a mother surrounded by two screaming boys to look as sexy and serene as your secretary, who probably spends at least an hour in front of the mirror before she comes to the office.'"

Sensing her anger rising, perhaps anger at herself for her lack of discipline, I said, "Sandy, how do you feel about your looks?"

She blushed and remained silent. Then with a friendly glance, she said, "I thought you were on my side."

"Did Gary ever complain about not having enough sex?"

"Oh, yes, he did but with a sense of humor. 'If I were meant to be celibate, I would have chosen to be a priest,' he said. I humored him. 'Find a tall, skinny blonde,' I said, not knowing then that he already had another woman on the side."

"It sounds that you paved the way."

"What do you mean?"

"You made it possible for him to find another woman."

"That's possible. We hardly talk anymore. He said I don't show interest in his work. He is an avid reader and I'm not. He bought me a couple of books, but I don't have time to read them. I prefer to watch my television shows."

"What do you think your message is to Gary?"

"He told me, 'Coming home is no longer the pleasure it used to be.' He finds me devoid of positive thoughts. 'I don't know what it will take to make you happy,' he said. And you know, Doctor, he's right. I'm not fun to be around. He probably finds me boring."

"Do you think that might be one of the reasons that he sought to fulfill himself with another woman?"

"Ask him. I think he was after more sex."

"Perhaps. If your husband is open to a new option, would you consider trying to be slim and shapely? Would you be interested in his work? Would you read the books he buys for you? Would you be a bit more cheerful when he comes home?"

"You're not asking for much, are you?" she asked sarcastically.

"I'm proposing a hypothesis: whatever Gary might desire in a new woman later, would he not rather have it in you now? Think about it."

"What if it's too late for changes?" she asked with genuine concern.

"Well, he hasn't packed his suitcases and moved out yet, has he?"

"No."

"Then changes are possible for both of you."

"But how can I compete with the other woman?"

"You don't have to. Just be who you are, but consider doing what she must have done to attract him."

"What did he see in her?" she asked.

"It's not what he saw in her; it's what she saw in him."

"I don't know what you mean."

The impact of the affair and her entangled emotions prevented Sandy from seeing her husband's needs. Of course she had needs of her own, but that's not what shuttled him into another woman's arms. Sandy needed some direction to regain inner peace, combat her own anxiety, and face the situation of her marriage.

Gary also needed to understand the responsibilities of married life. His escape into an affair did not necessarily provide a solution for his emotional needs. Unable to share his needs or ambitions with his wife, afraid of her disapproval, he distanced himself from the marriage.

The way spouses communicate personal or family needs to each other is a most basic issue. Appropriate timing and attitude play a major part when needs are being discussed. If the objective is to meet a need or to solve a problem, the dialogue ought to take place at a mutually agreeable time and in a good spirit. For example, try the following:

"I've something important to discuss with you. Is this a good time?"

This approach might have better results than if you say, "Sit down. I want to talk to you right now."

The first is a gentle invitation and it implies good intentions. The second is an order. It suggests control and power. Which one do you prefer?

When spouses are disenchanted with their marriage, they carry their dissatisfaction outside. Unconsciously and sometimes consciously, their faces reflect a sort of sadness or a need to talk to someone. If this someone happens to be of the other gender, divulging the dissatisfaction becomes much easier. Why? Not because this unique other shows empathy and understanding, but because, at that moment, male-female chemistry blends favorably. Nature complements the interaction. This lays the groundwork for the empathic listener to indulge in fantasy: "Poor baby; where have you been all my life? I can be good to you. I'll make you happy." In such reverie, the emotionally deprived partner accentuates his or her complaints about their marriage as the listener manifests genuine concern, and the plot thickens. The prelude to the affair is almost complete. Sailing to the island of fantasies leaves no time to consider the consequences of such involvement, at least initially.

When Gary came to see me alone, I realized what this other woman saw in him. Having been divorced herself, she saw in Gary a real man, the ideal for her. She admired his chic appearance and sense of humor. She showed sincere interest in Gary's work and complimented him on his innovative ideas. Gary mentioned a book he was reading, and before they met again, she had read that book and highlighted certain paragraphs that she was able to discuss with him. When he talked, she looked absorbed, reflecting interest in his message, encouraging him to continue talking about himself. The ingredients for a harmless relationship seemed right, and because he loved his wife and children, he was certain that nothing could go wrong, for he was in charge. Besides, who ever said that men cannot have women as friends? It's only an innocent friendship!

What happened to Gary? Unaware of an old proverb, "If your thoughts should take the wrong path even once, you will miss the right direction forever," his mind danced away on the stage of fantasy.

What started with a cup of coffee at Dunkin' Donuts evolved into a delicious dialogue over a luncheon at the Spanish Tavern. Seeing Gary's gourmet taste, she offered to make him a special dinner one evening at her apartment. Flattered and wanting to please her, he accepted the invitation.

Clean, serene, and fragrant, the stage was set and the props were in place: soft music, flowers, candlelight, a couple of books on the coffee table, and two champagne glasses. Dressed sexily, she greeted him at the door with a peck on the cheek and a warm welcome. Sensing his hesitation, she helped him to remove his coat and pointed to a comfortable couch. When she sat next to him, Gary could not help but notice her cleavage, and he felt a chemical reaction. Excited? Yes! Scared? Yes! But after the first glass of champagne, the healthy defenses lowered, lusty urges rose, nature responded. As if in a dream, Gary saw before him a woman so beautiful, so attractive, so noble, so altogether lovely. Her eyes sparkled with the joy of life, and a tender smile gave her face a beauty beyond comparison. Was it love at first sight? Whoever said that a man cannot love two women? Radiant, her velvety voice soothed his pounding heart. Clasping hands in a state of trance, they tiptoed toward the bedroom in slow motion, and the rest became history.

After the affair, what? How do you sit opposite your spouse and maintain a conversation? On his way home, Gary, deliciously exhausted, recollected his experience. He analyzed his thoughts. "I don't think Sandy really loves me. She probably needs me for the kids. I wonder if I really love her. She may agree with me that we don't love each other anymore so we should make a peaceful settlement." He felt hopeful.

When he arrived home feeling guilty, the sight of his wife and children shook him into the realization of the mess he had got himself into. Sandy had been to the beauty parlor in the afternoon, and she was wearing a new sleeveless dress. She looked pretty. The boys, unusually well disposed, wanted to spend the night at a friend's house and expected Daddy's permission.

"The boys have already eaten," she said. "We'll have dinner in fifteen minutes." Gary glanced around and smiled to disguise his inner turmoil. "How can I look Sandy and my children straight in the eye and tell them that I will no longer live with them because I'm going to start a new life with someone else? They haven't done anything wrong. What's wrong with me? Am I crazy?"

In the days that followed, Gary felt emotionally distant from Sandy and his home. Under the guise of deadlines he had to meet at work, he stayed away from his home for longer periods of time, leaving Sandy with suspicions. Initially, she kept asking him questions; then a friend advised her to hire a detective.

Oblivious to the possibility of being caught, Gary continued to see the other woman. He had developed strong feelings for her and enjoyed her company. He spent most of his evenings with her and told his wife he was busy at the office. His new friend had become a sort of addiction. He needed her. He decided that if something should happen to his wife, he would marry this woman almost immediately.

Afternoon delights and sexual siestas took their toll on him. He looked tired and sad. To his wife, who once believed that her husband was above this kind of life, he said, "I hate the rat race out there. I feel like running away." When she offered to get a job to relieve his pressure, he responded, "Forget it. It's not going to help."

Did Gary want to run away from his home responsibilities or from his involvement with the other woman who was making more claims upon his life? He began to question his own integrity, his own values, the lies he told his family, his own fluctuating thoughts. Although everything was not perfect at home, there was security, ownership, a sense of belonging. Sandy was fully involved with their children, but she still loved him in her own way. His children adored him.

He had worked hard to establish a home and have a family. He had shared years of history with Sandy. All of it was not bad. There were some healthy ingredients that kept their family together. He felt guilty abandoning what he had built over many years. He also felt guilty lying to his wife and improvising excuses for his absence.

In the presence of the other woman he had another set of feelings. Gorgeous, sexy, in his eyes she was pure joy and excitement. He envisioned a new life of romance and adventure. They developed projects together — she had some innovative ideas about advertising — they shared books and spent weekends together, but currents of guilt caused disturbing feelings of ambivalence that he attempted to drown with an additional glass of champagne.

Webster's dictionary defines ambivalence as "simultaneous attraction towards and repulsion from an object, person, or action." Caught in a state of ambivalence, Gary found himself attracted by two equally strong forces pointing toward different courses of action. Not knowing which way to go, what to decide, what to do, he felt confused. Unwilling to follow one direction or the other, he felt unable to give himself wholeheartedly to either and ran the risk of losing both. When Sandy discovered the affair, all hell broke loose. Gary was forced into a quick decision. As much as he loved the other woman and felt guilty because of the promises he had made to her, he decided to give her up and stay with his family. The difficult task of reconciliation was at hand. He had to adjust to not having the other woman any more and he missed her. Would he be able to invest some new loving feelings in his wife? Would he be faithful to her in the future? On the other hand, would his wife accept him? Would she be able to forgive and trust him again?

As we shall see in the next chapter, Gary had to go through therapy and personal transformation. To facilitate his recovery, I gave him the following directives:

1. Avoid the temptation to call, write, send presents to, or visit the other woman, if you want to have an affair-proof marriage.

2. Your thoughts about the other woman — that she is hurting and feeling lonely without you — are accurate. You have made a decision to repair your relationship with your wife; therefore, you cannot afford to look back. Allow the other woman to be an adult and seek healing on her own.

3. Giving the other woman a phone call to see how she is surviving the loss from her life will only rekindle romantic thoughts and hope in her. So don't call. Caring for her necessitates that you let time and God provide for a new direction.

4. Become more patient and gentle with your wife. Let her know that you understand how she feels. When you notice that she feels like talking, listen and try not to interrupt. She may disclose some of her deeper needs.

5. Get rid of old habits that annoy your wife. Call her during the day and find out how she feels. Show interest in what she does. Tell her what time you expect to be home. If you need to make plans that involve your wife, consult her and ask for her opinion. Don't surprise her with arbitrary and unilateral decisions. Simply inform her and make her feel important in your life.

Chapter 10

THE ART OF THE POSSIBLE

When you have wounded your partner deeply, you cannot expect instant improvement or miracle cures. It takes time and trust to rebuild a relationship.

— FLORENCE LITTAUER

If we consider the reality of relationships, be it a friendship or a marriage, we will agree that it takes sensitivity and caring, as well as good intentions and a genuine effort, to maintain a relationship. Otherwise, the relationship becomes anemic, withers, and eventually fades away.

Willing to work on his marriage, Gary returned to his wife. For two weeks he did not contact the other woman at all, and he felt relieved that he didn't have to make excuses or tell lies to his wife. Gently and patiently he spoke to his wife, acknowledging his violation and asking for her forgiveness. He reassured Sandy that his affair was over and that she had nothing to worry about.

Although still skeptical about her husband's honesty, Sandy tried diligently to apply the therapist's suggestions. She had decided that her marriage was important to her and gave evidence of cooperation. Periodically, as she recalled her husband's infidelity, her anger resurfaced, but she was careful not to remind him of his violation. Discussing her recurring thoughts with her therapist provided the needed comfort.

Despite his strong commitment to sever himself permanently from the affair, Gary's heart ached for the other woman. He wanted to see her, to talk to her, to be with her. A man of conscience in his search for a viable solution, he felt guilty about hurting his illicit lover. "I love her very much. I have promised her a great deal. How can I tell her that I'm going back to my family? What will she think of me?" Although he began to be more affectionate toward his wife and felt better about his decision to stay married to her, his mind gravitated toward the other woman. After all, they had a great deal in common, and they had shared many experiences; they had genuine feelings for each other and had visualized being married to each other some day. "Maybe God has destined us to be together," they thought. Besides, if he felt so good with her, if their relationship brought him so much joy, how could it be wrong to love this new woman who had come into his life?

Such rationalizations are not uncommon for people caught in a triangle. Gary could not totally understand that marital happiness cannot be divided into three equal portions. "There is no reason why I should not enjoy the situation for a while," he thought. "Why not? I may be the exception." By the end of the fourth week of absence from her, he had great difficulty in resisting the temptation to telephone her. "I just want to see how she is; that's not so terrible," he said to himself and dialed her number. His heart thrilled at hearing her voice. His body welled with anticipation.

"No, I cannot disappoint her, I must go to her for a little while. We can talk, but we don't have to make love." His heart palpitated intensely as he drove to her apartment. She was delighted to see him after four weeks of silence.

"What happened to you? I thought I had lost you for good. I felt abandoned," she said, her heart feeling again that rapturous torture she had felt when they first made love.

Gary remained silent, confused, and unable to discuss with her his decision to return to his wife and children. Nervously he smiled, but under that smile the echo of his own self-accusatory voice tormented him: "You are an adulterer...adulterer!" Feeling guilty, yet inviting more turmoil into his life, he looked at her with an oh-how-much-I-have-missed-you gleam in his eyes. He engulfed her in his arms and reminisced about the giddiness of secret meetings, of sharing small intimacies under the noses of others, of presents and surprises, of their spontaneous out-of-town escapades. How often they had dared such an exciting life in months past! To do so again was dangerous, Gary thought, especially now that his wife knew about the affair. Yet the idea seduced him in a way that made him feel more vibrant, more alive than he had been since the last time they had been together.

After the rekindling of the relationship, between doubt about his decision to stay married to his wife and the desire to be with the other woman, Gary asked me with the sincere innocence of a child, "Doctor, please tell me why I feel this way about this other...?"

In the way some therapists usually respond, I said, "Why do you think you feel this way?"

"She's so great. I feel happy in her presence, and I know I love her a lot. We could have an exciting marriage together."

As I listened to Gary describing the details of his romance, I pondered how unaware he was of the instincts created by God in all human beings. With genuine compassion I said, "Gary, I want you to consider the invisible forces that operate within you and your friend. It is the same creative force that you felt within you when you fell in love with your wife. As well as the evident attraction you have for this other woman which, like a magnet, continues to pull you together, God's plan for propagating humanity is in operation."

As if I were speaking another language, Gary said curiously, "I don't know what you mean."

"Nature wants babies."

"I don't plan to father any more children," he said seriously.

"What about your friend?"

"She agreed with me that we don't need to have children as long as we have each other."

"And you believe her?"

"I do. I do."

"Then why don't you bite the bullet — marry her?"

"What about my wife and children? How are they going to feel?" He sighed deeply. "What are they going to think of me?" Evident pain moistened his eyes. Empathic in the presence of heartbreak, silently I asked myself, "Is this love? I thought love ought to make people happy."

Gary's conflict is not uncommon among people who undulate between two partners. Unable to invest their emotions in one spouse, they succumb to a life of split loyalties and torment. Unless you are a circus performer, you cannot ride two horses at the same time. Even if you are a performer, in order for you to keep your balance, the horses need to go in a circle, otherwise you fall.

Afraid he might fall and lose his romantic adventure as well as his family, Gary, like the circus artist, kept going around in circles. When he was with his wife, he felt good about his decision to stay married. Besides, he perceived her to be a good person, and she had not done anything wrong to deserve a divorce. But when he visited his other friend, his thoughts about staying married to Sandy were shaken. "My marriage is good, comfortable, but it is lukewarm." The potential of making a new marriage seemed very exciting. "Why not? Darn it, we only live once! I deserve the best!"

Under such romantic intoxication, does anyone really know what is the best? The best for whom? For Gary? For his wife? For the other woman? In a state of persistent confusion, undecided about which way to go, he indulged in the fantasy that he needed time out to filter his feelings.

"A man needs time to figure out what to do with his life."

"You're right," I said. "You need time to process your thoughts, your feelings, your own reality, but how much time do you think you need?"

After a moment of silence, he said, "Oh, I need at least ninety days."

Knowing that procrastination and indecision conspire against a viable solution, I asked, "Why ninety?"

"I really can't make up my mind at this time. I need time so I can make a good decision."

A little humor, I thought, might diffuse Gary's ambivalence. "Aesop tells the story of a middle-aged man who had a wife and a relationship with a younger woman. Each woman loved him very much and wished his appearance suited her own age. His hair began to turn gray — a fact that the younger woman did not like, for it made him look too old to be her husband. Each time they met, she managed to comb his hair and pluck out the white ones. His wife, being older, was pleased to see her husband going gray, for she did not want to be mistaken for his mother. Every morning, she volunteered to comb his hair, and as she did so, she pulled out as many black hairs as she could. Eventually, the man found himself entirely bald."

Gary smiled and said, "I think I get the message. Aesop's fable makes it clear. If I yield to the wishes of both women, sooner or later I will have nothing to yield. I have to make a choice."

Weeks later, when Gary came to see me for the fifth time, it occurred to me that he had made a choice. Evidence of interest in his wife's well-being — taking her out for dinner, planning a vacation with her in the Caribbean Islands, spending more time with her, and making himself purposely unavailable to the other woman — convinced me that the scale was heavier on the side of his marriage. He appeared more at peace, although the implementation of his decision seemed difficult. He wanted to fade out of the other woman's life smoothly, possibly without hurting her.

It is not uncommon for us to make decisions in our subconscious mind a long time before we make them available to ourselves or to others. However, procrastination and indecision reinforce each other and most of the time lead to failure or depression.

Instead of providing further details regarding the development of Gary and Sandy's married life — which could easily occupy another volume — it may be of greater benefit to discuss areas that both partners had to work on for their individual growth and the development of their relationship.

I asked Gary how he planned to use his ninety days, and he replied that he would leave things alone and would work on himself. "Be a bit more specific," I said, and he replied, "I'll give my marriage the best shot."

"What about the other woman?"

"I won't see her as often, and I'll be very discreet."

"Not good enough," I said. "To do justice to yourself and to your wife, you will have to let go of the other totally."

"Totally? You're asking the impossible. What if I lose her?"

"Well, you cannot lose someone who is not your own. Besides, you said you want to give your marriage the best shot? Correct?"

"Yes, I did say that. I love my wife."

"So let's try to work on the art of the possible."

"I don't know what you mean."

"The art of the possible is the ability that we have to make things happen for us, for example, to create healthy and productive relationships. This ability is inherent in all humans. If you want to develop a relationship with your wife and truly live a fulfilled, self-actualized life, you need to accept complete responsibility for the way you choose to go about relating to her. This, like other areas of a good life, may require that you unlearn old habits, renounce expectations, and acquire a willingness to believe in the art of the possible."

In a situation like Gary's, you can have a loving and fulfilling relationship with your partner if you apply the following basic points:

~ Let go of the other lover for ninety days while you are clarifying your thoughts and understanding your feelings. There are to be no phone calls, no meetings, no contacts; otherwise you will be wasting your time and your money seeking the help of a therapist.

~ Cultivate your partner's trust in you by being emotionally and physically present in your partner's life. This does not mean that you quit your job to become always available. Rather, it means that when you are together, you must be there with a positive attitude. A gentle touch, an attentive ear, a sense of humor, a helping hand, a back massage — all these your partner will love. Share an experience and periodically say, "I love you."

~ Watch your avoidance patterns which include ignoring needs, avoiding participation in domestic tasks, avoiding or even forgetting to do things that you promised to do — even simple things such as taking the car to the garage to have the oil changed or calling the plumber to fix the leaking pipe in your bathroom. Things that you consider unimportant and expect your partner to take care of — leaving your shoes under the dining room table or your underwear on the floor — indicate a lack of responsibility and a lack of respect.

~ Refrain from controlling your partner's life. Allow your partner to be who he or she is and encourage and praise activities. Using arrogant, angry, or abusive language is like dripping poison into emotional veins. Think: "This is the person I love, and I want this person to love me." Ignoring feelings, using harsh words, making demands, finding fault, pointing an accusing finger — such behavior will make you an adversary and will increase the distance between the two of you.

~ If you notice that your partner is reacting negatively to your well-intentioned efforts, allow some time to pass and wait for feelings to cool. Then, explain your intentions and ask your partner to suggest a better way to approach the situation. If you resort to "Nothing that I do or say pleases my partner," then it is time to reexamine what it is that you are doing or saying.

~ Make loving gestures, such as a phone call during the day to see how your partner feels, an occasional bouquet of flowers, a special dinner, an unexpected present. All these reminders promote good will and convey feelings of love.

An old saying claims, "The mirror only reflects the way we look into the mirror." Give love and you will receive love.

~ FOUR ~

COMMUNICATE
AND CONNECT

*"Communicate" literally means to become one with,
to make a heart-to-heart connection
that gives evidence of who we are
and who the other is.*

⌒⧒⌒

*Don't fear that you might be misunderstood
or even criticized.
Welcome it!*

Chapter 11

HOW TO RELATE

In sharing ourselves with others, we must always take full responsibility for our own thoughts, feelings, actions and reactions. — JOHN POWELL

When we meet, we shake hands, a customary exchange of greeting or a form of acceptance that sets the stage for dialogue. It is in dialogue that we discover the other. Through it, we understand and are understood. Through it, we select friends and partners. What determines the course of further interaction depends upon our ability to relate with each other. Life becomes significant the moment we look into another's eyes. The handshake or smile clears the air. It is a reassurance that neither of us holds a weapon to hurt the other. We are free to start a relationship. The communication process begins.

Did you ever choose to be alone? Perhaps you wanted time out to think things through, to take a personal inventory of your life. Many people do that; they cut out some of the distractions to simplify their life, to rest, relax, meditate. We can say it is a good feeling, a state of strength and grace, but how long can we truly remain alone without becoming lonely? We were created to be with other people. It is in the presence of people that we feel validated and alive, and we sense the need to say something to confirm each other's life.

Since the beginning of your life, you were able to relate with your environment, initially your caretakers and later your significant others. Most likely you have developed a style of talking to other people that is familiar and comfortable to you. If your style works for you and is effective, why would you change it? Perhaps you might like to improve it. This chapter will offer some guidelines that you might consider as you reach out to relate with other people.

A very important step in reaching out to make contact is to accept yourself, your own reality. Initially, you might hesitate. Thoughts like the following may race through your mind:

~ How much of me should I reveal? Do I need to be transparent?

~ What will happen when my less desirable qualities surface?

~ What if the other person doesn't like me or even rejects me?

Such questions are inevitable. They tell us we are human, and in certain areas we feel insecure. In not reaching out to relate with another human being, either because of fear that we might not be accepted or because we are afraid to reveal our insecurities, we deprive ourselves of an opportunity to establish a relationship. Think about it. No one has to be a very special person, a celebrity, or a hero to relate with another. We don't need additional muscles, a face lift, a change of color, height, age, sex, intelligence, or wealth.

We need to come to terms with who we are and accept the person that we are. Say, "I am who I am. This is the real me." Learning to access and accept our inner self is a big part of communications. Once we do this, then accepting the other is much easier. The other person is also a human being endowed with human strengths and weaknesses. Accepting the other person without expectations that she or he must agree with us or live the same style of life as we do lays a solid foundation for a good relationship. As we interact honestly and warmly with another person, we discover a new dimension of ourselves.

Also important is the ability to distinguish between surface and substance. It's not always easy to separate the apparent from the inherent. Put in simple terms, words can be superficial and vacuous or they can be sincere and meaningful. While you learn about others, do you want to impress them with your presence or do you want to share your life? It is easy to pass judgment on a polished manner, a pleasing face, sweet words, and a well-chosen wardrobe — each of which is good to possess — but there is more to life and to people than appearances. Of course appearances are impressive, but after the first minute of contact, it is prudent to transcend the appearance and see the person. You have a choice to make: a heart-to-heart talk or a superficial exchange. Naturally, we want to feel important and we want to be recognized by others. This depends upon you as you indicate what kind of conversation you wish to encourage. It also depends upon the other person, who indicates how receptive and willing he or she is to talk.

Suppose that Ben and Joe meet at the YMCA. Both members sit by the swimming pool. Consider their conversation:

Ben: Hi Joe!
Joe: Hi!
Ben: That's a great suntan you have. Were you on vacation?
Joe: Yeah.
Ben: Where did you go?
Joe: Backyard.
Ben: Do you have a garden?
Joe: Yep.
Ben: Flowers?
Joe: Tomatoes.
Ben: Do you enjoy gardening?
Joe: I guess so.

Is there anything more frustrating than trying to strike up a conversation with someone who responds in monosyllables? It's like pulling teeth. If this is aggravating with acquaintances or colleagues, imagine how frustrating it is trying to connect with an important person in your life. Granted that some people have a hard time talking with others. Either they lack the emotional component of the conversation or the vocabulary. Possibly they are afraid to reveal who they really are, or, simply, they may not want to talk. If their self-esteem is low or nonexistent, they may think that what they have to say is worthless. "I'm a big nothing. I don't feel like talking to anybody. Who would listen to me anyhow?" Such thinking would make relating cumbersome.

Another barrier to communication is the thought that, "If I open up to you, I may burden you." Some individuals have similar thoughts, although a different perspective. "People don't want to hear about me. They have enough problems of their own."

To sustain a good conversation, you have to know what to say. In order to know what to say, you have to get in touch with those deep-inside-of-you feelings, thoughts, needs, and wishes. These are integral parts of your personality.

If you are protective of what is inside you, because you feel embarrassed or ashamed or guilty, then, as you relate with the other, your conversation might remain shallow, without substance. Remember, when you start a conversation you don't have to reveal everything within you — personal history or family secrets — to keep the communication going. Just be genuinely present at that moment.

Talking, like walking, may seem automatic, as when a person babbles on about anything and anybody. When you talk about things that really matter, when you are emotionally present, however, you will discover beauty and grace in yourself and in the other. It takes some effort and skill, but if you try you will be rewarded.

In sharing your thoughts and feelings with another, you make communication possible for yourself, which helps to nurture a relationship. Any time two people are together, each has an experience that affects the other in some way. The experience can serve to reinforce, either positively or negatively, what is expected. It may create doubts about the other's worth and thus create distrust, or it may deepen and strengthen the worth of each, and the trust and the closeness increases. Every interaction between two people has a powerful impact on the respective worth of each and what happens between them.

Visualize a couple who, in their daily interaction, begin to feel doubts about and distance from each other. To gain a feeling of worth for themselves, they begin to look elsewhere — to work, to children, to other partners. If a husband and wife begin to have sterile and lifeless encounters, they eventually become bored with one another. Boredom leads to indifference, one of the worst of human feelings and, incidentally, one of the real causes of divorce. I'm convinced that anything exciting, even if it is risky, is preferable to boredom. A fair argument is better than boredom. The two might hurt each other's feelings momentarily, but at least they feel alive while it's going on. Once their aggression subsides, they can start talking to each other in a more mature manner.

Styles We Use to Communicate

Submissive persons may unintentionally encourage a relationship to be lopsided. Hesitant or unable to express their feelings in a forthright way, they may agree with or placate the other person, giving the impression that the other's behavior does not matter. They are eager to please, never disagreeing, always wanting the other to approve of them. Having a diminished sense of self-worth, they allow the other to violate their inner space.

Faultfinders, those who are not pleased with anything or anybody, have a hard time relating. They may be pointing a finger accusingly, throwing their weight around, unwilling to hear any response. Inside, they may feel worthless, but if they get someone to agree with them, they may feel that they count for something.

There are some who choose the longest words possible to impress the other and find it difficult to relate to the average person. After the initial talk, they may find themselves alone and lonely.

Competing characters are not listeners. They hear what is being said but in their mind they compare it to what they think is better. While all their mental measuring is going on, they may be clever enough to fake facial expressions and verbal responses. They tolerate what is said only so that they can look down on another; in reality they don't want to know the other.

Distracters are people who diffuse and confuse relationships. Unable to remain focused on the conversation, they interrupt or complete somebody else's sentences. What they say is irrelevant to what anyone else is saying or doing. They never make a response to the point.

If you find yourself in any of the above descriptions, you probably learned this way of relating early in your life. As you tried to make your way through the complicated and often threatening world in which you found yourself, you used one or another of these means of relating. You may have heard well-intentioned advice like the following:

~ "Don't impose; it's selfish to ask for things for yourself." This helps to reinforce placating.

~ "Don't let anyone put you down; don't be a coward." This helps to reinforce blaming.

~ "Don't be so serious. Live it up! Who cares?" This helps to reinforce distracting.

These are some of the crippling modes of relating ingrained in us from childhood.

On the other hand, there is a positive and productive approach that builds bridges between people and heals ruptures. When you use this approach, you level with others. Even if you want to apologize for something that you did not intend, you are apologizing for an act, not for your existence. There are times when you need to criticize and evaluate. When you do so in a leveling way, you are evaluating an act, not blaming the person, and there is usually a new direction you have to offer.

The positive person can be real. When she says, "I like you," her voice is warm and she looks at you. If her message is, "I'm angry with you," her voice is harsh and her face tight. A positive person who levels with another represents honesty and truth at the moment of the interaction.

Let's take an imaginary situation. I'm your neighbor, and you park your car near to my driveway in such a way that I have a hard time getting my car in and out. The following are different ways that I could approach my neighbor:

Submissive: "Hi, Donald. I'm ... uh ... gee, I ... am sorry ... you feeling okay? You know ... promise me you won't get mad ... no, it's just ... maybe you can park your car a little better? Just a little, maybe? Hm?"

Blaming: "For God's sake, Don, don't you know how to park a car? Why don't you take some parking lessons?"

Impressing: "I have perused our entire neighborhood. Not a single car has been parked as awkwardly as the Cherokee, namely, yours. Would you care to make any comment?"

Distracting (talking to another neighbor who happens to be passing by): "Say, Fred, do you park your car like Donald here does? No, there is really nothing wrong with his parking — I was just walking around the neighborhood. Tell Don to stop by the motor vehicle bureau and sign up for lessons."

Positive-assertive: "Don, I have a hard time entering my driveway, because of the way you park your car. You have been doing it all this week, and I don't want to cause any damage to your car. We need to stop, take a look, and see if there's a safer parking spot."

It's not easy to break old patterns and relate with other people in a leveling way. Once you get in touch with the fears that hinder your ability to relate, however, you will be more eager to reach out. What are these fears and how can we deal with them?

~ You might make a mistake, *but* all humans make mistakes.

~ Someone might not like you, *but* everyone doesn't have to like you.

~ Someone might criticize you, *but* some criticism can be useful.

~ You might impose, *but* any time you talk to another person you impose.

~ Someone might think you are no good, *but* you have good qualities.

~ You might be thought of as a fraud, *but* it only matters what you think of yourself.

~ You might be rejected, *but* although nobody wants to be rejected, we endure it.

When you find it difficult to connect with another person, do not think of yourself as abnormal. It is difficult to immerse yourself in another person's world. All of us stand by our own perceptions. The perceptions of another can be affirmed by responding with our authentic self and conveying appreciation and regard, thus enabling the other person to feel fully human.

An aggressive person may overpower the other by controlling or monopolizing the conversation. A narcissistic type of talk — that is, relating our own accomplishments, aspirations, successes, and grandiose plans without allowing the other to insert a word — may bore or arouse jealously or anger in the listener. The message conveyed is: This is who I am; this is what I want; who you are and what you want are of lesser importance to me — or of no importance at all. An aggressive approach to any relationship, regardless of where it originates, makes manipulation inevitable. The exploitation continues until the listener rejects us and moves away.

Assertive persons, on the other hand, maintain self-respect by pursuing the satisfaction of their needs and safeguarding boundaries without abusing or dominating or invading the privacy of others. Such behavior implies that we possess confidence and acceptance of who we are — human beings with abundant qualities, strengths, and weaknesses. As mature adults, we develop healthy defense mechanisms that enable us to face people and situations with a sense of boldness, without chips on our shoulders. With inner confidence, we do not have to start a war to defend our position. We are entitled to a lifestyle of our choice, and, while we maintain our convictions, we do not have to impose them on others. Allowing others to unfold in their unique ways, without making judgments, and responding with undivided attention show others that we care for them.

Relationships have limitations. We cannot expect to feel deep interest in every individual we meet. Our time is too short and our emotional resources are not sufficient for casual dispersal among mere acquaintances. At least, we can be courteous. How much time and how much energy do we have to demonstrate sincere interest and concern for others? In a family setting we experience lasting relationships. Outside the family circle we may have a few intimate friends with whom we keep the barriers to a deep of relationship low.

Peripheral to the close friends, there are probably individuals with whom we are closely associated in business or in other well-defined areas of common interest. An awareness of each other's boundaries makes interaction viable. There are areas in the lives of most of us that are rightfully opened only to a select few and areas where no one is permitted. The fact that such areas exist must be accepted, understood, and respected.

For Your Consideration

~ Create a friendly climate. Make sure that the other person is ready to listen.

~ Don't approach the other person with an argumentative attitude; if you do, the other person will find it difficult to talk to you.

~ Don't insist that the other person is wrong, implying that you are right; to do so forces the person to take a protective or even a polemic attitude.

~ If a person's self-esteem is threatened, don't disagree with or put that person down.

~ Avoid criticizing or threatening others. State your disagreements in terms of personal thoughts or opinions.

~ Be positive. Most people are attracted to and interested in positive things. A negative approach turns them off. It is just as easy to say, "walk around the edge," as to say, "avoid the water."

~ Be clear. A clear and concise statement won't make others accept your point of view, but at least they will be able to understand it. Understanding is necessary for acceptance.

~ Be simple. To make a healthy contact, use short, simple, everyday words. Many people know the meaning of "prevaricator" but everyone knows the meaning of "liar."

~ Maintain interest. You may have a useful idea that others fail to see. Find the area of usefulness and remind them of the use. They may accept your idea. If they don't, it doesn't mean your idea is not good.

~ When people you are talking to wander off the subject, bring their attention back by a probe such as "Do you see any problem with what I'm talking about?" By asking a question, you relate to their psychological need for freedom to speak. At the same time, you are exercising psychological leverage by bringing them back to the topic you want to discuss.

YOUR POTENTIAL

To achieve your potential, there must be at least one other person with whom you are totally open and you feel totally safe at the same time. — PAUL TOURNIER

We are usually attracted to people who speak the same language as we do, who communicate with us on same wavelength, who accept us and show interest in what we do, and we enjoy sharing with them our thoughts and feelings. We feel reasonably comfortable in their company. In the process, as we show interest in their activities, we learn about their life and share their interests.

On the other hand, there are people in whose presence we feel uncomfortable. Something occurs within us as we meet them, and after a lukewarm, "Hi," we have nothing more to say; we move on unaffected. The same thing might be occurring on their side.

Meaningful contact is a human need. Contact comes when we sense the difference we make to other people and the difference they make to us as we meet. However, when we meet others without really talking to them, we fail to reveal our inner richness. Think about this for a moment. As you reach out to connect with a significant other, you are extending emotional hospitality. You are actually inviting someone to share part of yourself.

If you want your partner to stop guessing about your feelings and motives, you have to be prepared to reveal yourself. And in order to reveal yourself, you have to know yourself. You can't talk openly and honestly with another until you have tried being honest with yourself first. Get in touch with your own feelings and become aware of what is going on inside you. Take time off to be alone. Use that time not simply to engage in passive meditation, but to carry on an active inner dialogue with yourself, between the person you think you are and the inner you that operates at gut level, the part of you that is real and honest. Communicating with yourself involves revelation, self-analysis, and reevaluation. You can't effectively convey your thoughts unless your thoughts are clear to you. You can't really communicate your feelings intelligently to another person unless you are ready to try to understand them yourself.

"Can I do all that?" you may ask. It is an honest question that many people ask frequently. My honest answer is, "Yes, you can."

After forty-four years of dealing with people, I have seen many in despair, living dull and dreary lives, who suddenly recognize their hidden possibilities, learn how to develop their latent potential, and find that their relationships can come alive and start to grow. This has happened and continues to happen in my practice of psychotherapy with couples receiving counseling. There is an immense amount of human potential that is never appropriated. I'm inclined to think that Einstein's guess about people using only 10 percent of their intellectual potential might apply equally to all relationships, including marriage. People run away from each other, overtly or covertly afraid to face the challenge of using their potential, of sharing the richness of their soul.

Sit across from me for a moment. Relax and let's focus on the present condition of your relationship. You are not happy; you have thought of separation or even divorce and now you have second thoughts. You are still exploring your own qualities and the potential of your relationship. You don't want to break off what started with enthusiasm and love. You are considering alternatives. We need to concentrate on what you can do to make this relationship satisfactory and predictably fulfilling for yourself and your partner. Can you do it alone? Not really, but you can improve your situation significantly when you do your part well.

What would you do if you were terribly embittered by your partner, and you didn't want to trust, reconcile, or enter another relationship ever again? Let's answer this common question with another equally significant question: What kind of life do you expect for yourself if you hold on to your bitterness and to your damaged emotions?

This was Kathy's experience when she began to distrust the people in her life. She retreated into a private world of questioning and doubting, searching for an answer to the deceit, manipulation, and betrayal that surrounded her at work and in her neighborhood. Five years before, her husband had abandoned her and married his secretary. Angry and heartbroken, Kathy decided not to remarry. "I won't trust another man," she said. She diffused her loneliness by becoming involved with her only daughter, who had just entered middle school. At a PTA meeting, Kathy met Joseph, a handsome young man whose wife had died of cancer two years before, leaving him with a boy of her daughter's age. Discussion about their children and common interests led them into a casual relationship. They met socially a few times. Joseph took Kathy to an elegant restaurant and introduced her to oriental delicacies. To reciprocate his kindness, she invited him to her home for dinner. Gradually their relationship became serious, and they fell passionately in love with each other. One evening, over a romantic dinner, he asked her to marry him. Although excited by the idea, an inner force held her back from saying yes. Joseph was ten years younger, and although she had strong feelings for him, she hesitated to marry a younger man. Her daughter, who had met Joseph on several occasions, encouraged her mother: "Marry him, Mommy; he's a good man." Eventually Kathy said yes, and soon he and his son moved into her house. Both thought this was a family made in heaven. The wedding date was left undefined. "We love each other . . . we can marry any time we want," they agreed.

Joseph traveled periodically. He was a good negotiator, and his company sent him to different parts of the country on business. On one of his California trips, he stayed longer than usual. Proud of his success, Kathy didn't think much of his absence. "Business is business." She made no negative remarks, but she realized that Joseph seemed preoccupied and distant. She asked him if anything was wrong. He replied that he was thinking about a new project and he had to go to California again. Kathy congratulated him on being held in such high esteem by his company.

Late one night, a phone call woke them up. Joseph tumbled out of bed and took the phone call in the next room. Kathy had a feeling that something was wrong. Intuition joined suspicion, and she did something she never thought she would do. She picked up the extension in another room and listened. The conversation was romantic and shockingly revealing. Kathy's night became a nightmare. In the early morning when she confronted him, he responded angrily that nobody had the right to control his life. As she probed, he admitted that while in Los Angeles, he had met an old flame he had known before he had married his first wife. They were high school sweethearts in Spain; he left her behind when he decided to come to America. She was a year younger than he and attending UCLA for postgraduate studies. Now he realized how much he really loved her.

In a subdued and hurt voice Kathy asked, "What do you think you want to do about this?"

He said, "I'm confused . . . I still have strong feelings for her."

"Then go to her," she said angrily and ran into the next room to hide her tears.

The story ended as Joseph and his son moved out and found residence with his parents. Meanwhile, Kathy had to deal with a broken promise and a broken dream. She cried a lot and blamed herself for choosing men who abandoned her. She sought therapy to soothe her pain and searched for answers in her inner self. She wanted to live honestly, but she no longer knew where or how to begin.

She was isolated, withdrawn, alone. Her darkness increased and the fear of total dissipation of self overwhelmed her. Her daughter spent most of her leisure time with friends. Kathy began to feel that nothing mattered; her body stiffened. Work became a boring routine. Some days she remained in her room and preferred to stay under the covers.

Then one day a friend who truly cared about Kathy approached her. The betrayal and pain were her own, yet Kathy could also feel the human presence of someone who loved her, someone who would not interfere. Their communication was silent and wordless, yet a bond began to grow between them. Slowly, Kathy began to weep; her tears flowed freely, her body awakened, and for the first time in many months, she felt movement and life. Her breathing deepened. She was connected with another human being in a way that she felt to be real. She had made a contact that she knew she could trust. None of the old patterns would ever be the same; the break with them was complete, but the feeling was not one of desperation or helplessness.

It was a touching moment when she felt the compassion and love of another person and knew she could begin again. She made a new start that took her out of her room into the sunshine where she felt more energy and a desire to live. Her gradual healing brought her, unafraid, in contact with other people, though at first only with individual members of her family. Soon she began to live in accordance with her real self, and this was all that mattered.

In a recent session, Kathy said, "I'm at peace with myself. I know there is life out there, and there are people out there. Some of them are benevolent. One of them might be a better companion for me, even a husband. I think I would like that, but the relationship would have to be honest and real, a bonding that we both would work on and both enjoy. If something like that never happens, I will not have a problem enjoying whatever I have attained in my life thus far."

What I witnessed in Kathy's evolution was a yearning to work diligently and to live honestly in the present. She entertained no regrets about the past, no pipe dreams or fantasies about the future, but a desire to use body, soul, and spirit for a healthier present. Her potential to face her dilemma had been there, but she had to go through the process of healing.

Life without obstacles and problems is inconceivable. You probably have had your share of obstacles already. If I were to tell you that, as of this hour, your life was going to be smooth sailing, with no conflicts or problems on the way, I would be lying to you. Unexpected events may throw you off balance or cause lasting pain. However, your potential to face adversity and advance in life is also there, within you. Regardless of what your experiences have been thus far, whether your parents divorced, or one of them died when you were a child, or you grew up in a hostile environment and you feel you are a victim of mental and physical abuse, there is hope.

Obstacles to Communication

Have you ever met a person whom you wanted to know or with whom you desired to develop a friendship, but with whom you had a hard time holding a conversation? Sometimes there are things that hold us back from becoming close to others. When you are about to make a contact with another person, how do you feel inside? Is there a tremor of hesitation? Do you feel that you have nothing to talk about? Some people do. This is also true about

some people who are close and have the same thoughts and feelings, week in and week out. To "speak freely" means saying and
hearing the same old stuck phrases from the same stuck places.
This can be boring.

Often obstacles in life take the form of inhibitions, which cloud
our minds, restrain our growth, and prevent us from reaching
out. We may respond to others, but in ways that are anemic,
inappropriate, lukewarm, or even negative.

Fear is one such inhibiting factor. It is a risk to let someone
get to know you. You are letting someone see you as you are and
risking that that person will reject what they see. If you have been
rejected in the past and fear that this should happen again, you can
lessen your fear by concentrating more and convincing yourself of
your own worth so that you can afford to take that risk, one step
at a time. Consider the possibility that a person who rejects you
may have problems of which you are not aware.

If you feel inferior to others or if you feel sorry for yourself,
thinking and feeling that you lack looks, brains, talent, or wealth,
you might stay away from people. If that's how you perceive yourself, you might think that others would find it difficult to come
closer to you.

Envy and jealousy are definite obstacles that can prevent you
from reaching out. Envy is an unpleasant feeling directed toward
another person's good fortune or success. It is a result of comparing your unhappiness to the joy of others. When your neighbor's
grass appears greener, then envy is settling in your mind and
distorting your thinking.

Sometimes wanting to have what others have or desiring to be
like them causes resentment and avoidance. You may even find
that others are jealous of you. This, too, can be a barrier in getting
to know people, but the jealousy of others is their problem, and
they will have to learn to deal with it on their own. Rather than
simply responding with resentment, perhaps you might try a more
positive approach, such as pointing out a good quality that they
might have. Try to see others as people, not as idealized images of
giants. Remember that others feel the need to be accepted, liked,
and respected.

Suppose you start with acquaintances. Certainly you want to
experience them in their inner reality. Vice versa, you want your

reality to be noticed and actually sensed by the other person. If you have experienced something exciting and share it with others who are merely acquaintances, your experience may seem almost dull to them. It may be wise to keep it safe inside you, untold. In that way it won't shrivel up and lose all the meaning it has for you.

Next, start with a friend. If you share something exciting with a real friend, it becomes more exciting. A good story will expand; you will find yourself telling it in more detail, feeling the flow of your vocabulary, finding the richness of the elements, more than when you thought about it alone. If it is a joyful event then your joy will be doubled; if it is a sad experience, your sadness will significantly diminish.

The axiom, "If anything good is to happen, it has to start with me," is a very productive approach. Become a good listener. When you enter the company of another person, after the initial greeting and exchange of amenities, set a few minutes aside when you only listen. You will discover that others will tell you much more about themselves, and you will be eager to share a lot more about yourself. Your eye contact, facial expression, and verbal affirmations such as, "I see," or "Oh, that's very interesting," or "No wonder you feel that way," or "I want to hear more about this; what an experience!" or "I lost you; can you say that again, please?" will enliven the talk. If you lose interest or you feel it's time for you to speak, you could say, "When you finish, I have a story to tell you."

Some thirty-five years ago, I learned a lasting lesson from a poet, Kimon Friar. I wanted to meet him, so while in Athens, I initiated a phone call that went like this:

Peter Kalellis: Mr. Friar, I have heard a lot about you, and I want to meet you.

Kimon Friar: That would be very nice. Today, at 4:00 p.m., I plan to be at Zonar's, a coffee shop near Constitution Square.

PK: I know exactly where that is. I could meet you there.

KF: Fine. I'll tell you a little bit about myself, and you can tell me a little bit about yourself. It should be fun.

We met that afternoon, and he spoke for about ten minutes about himself, and then with a smile, he said, "Your turn." We spent more than two hours together, sharing our aspirations, he about his poetry and I about my writing; it was a most pleasant experience, a dialogue that gave the impression of a tennis game in very slow motion. Pleasantly, we shook hands and parted, but that brief encounter initiated a friendship that lasted for many years. The lesson that remains with me is that if someone monopolizes the conversation, gently step in and say something like this, "Let's come back to your story in a couple of minutes, because there is something that I want to share with you, and I don't want to forget it." Or "When you finish, there is something I have to share with you." Such an interruption is not offensive; on the contrary, it relieves the other for a few minutes while you take an active part in the conversation.

"In spite of what you are telling me, I find it very difficult to connect with people," Larry said with sad eyes. "I have just come back from an out-of-town conference. It was a disaster. I was looking forward to going to it, but once I got there, I couldn't find anyone to talk to." Understandably, in a strange environment with strangers all around, it might be difficult to start talking to someone without some initial anxiety. If there is an inner fragmentation and you feel insecure, then anything that comes out of your mouth will suffer. Don't underestimate yourself; you are not transparent and nobody can look into your innermost thoughts to discover how you feel. You can still strike up a decent conversation. Suppose you start with a smile, introduce yourself, and try to keep the focus off yourself. In your conversation, concentrate on what the other person is saying, then respond with a sentence that begins with "You" rather than "I."

For example, if someone begins to talk about a car accident, don't respond with a story about your car accident experience. Instead, say something that either paraphrases what the other person said or that shows that you really heard the story. You might say, "You really had a scary experience, didn't you?"

This is called active listening. You will be pleasantly surprised at how much you learn and how purposeful you feel. This is the way to start utilizing your own potential in communications.

For Your Consideration

~ Think of yourself not as a man or a woman but as a human being endowed with strengths and weaknesses, a person who possesses a potential that can be tapped and improved.

~ Evaluate the good qualities and aspects of your personality that you like, and make a plan to use them constructively. Keep your negative qualities in check for a while, until you are able to deal with them in a nondestructive way.

~ Past memories, especially hurtful ones, are like bad tenants. Replace them with plans for today and convince yourself that the past cannot change, but can serve as a lesson not to be repeated.

~ As you talk to others do not play yourself down or refer to yourself with "bad" adjectives. Denigrating yourself to humor others or to solicit sympathy will stifle your potential to connect with other people.

~ If you make an effort to start a conversation and someone criticizes what you say, do not interpret it as a personal attack. If the criticism has merit, use it for personal improvements.

~ Whether you are wife or husband, mother or father, single, married, divorced, or widowed, enjoy that stage. Our life is like a long journey with many stops. Cherish each stop on the way and get hold of whatever it offers.

~ As you enter a conversation, think of what you are able to offer and decide what you are able to receive. Develop a conversation that is pleasing, without paranoid overprotection of yourself.

~ Start a conversation as you would start a walk, one step at a time. If you feel pressure, pause and explore the possibility of "power struggle." There is no reason to play tit-for-tat so that you might win. It is a wasted effort that hinders your growth.

~ As you relate with others, be flexible enough to negotiate or treat them with courtesy and concern. Then your potential to connect with others will develop quickly.

Chapter 13

LOVING COMMUNICATION

We want to share our lives with someone who loves us unconditionally. We want to grow old with a partner who has valued us, understood us, and helped us feel safe in sharing our deepest feelings and needs. — GARY SMALLEY

Good communication is an absolute must for couples who intend to stay together. Communication implies more than an average conversation; it is an exchange of loving thoughts and feelings. It is amazing what happens when there is love in our lives. We talk, we touch, we hug, we hold, we satisfy each other's needs. As a result, we experience emotional security, self-worth, creativity, energy, productivity, joy, and a sense of roots — belonging somewhere.

Loving communication is a result of a loving relationship. When we feel love in our hearts, we find communication to be a rewarding experience. You may have noticed that when you are in good spirits, your ability to speak to someone is better. You are also able to listen without interrupting others, allowing them to finish their thoughts. When you have peace and joy in your heart, your thoughts are congruent, your words are coherent, your voice is firm and clear. You feel good about what you are saying, and you are content to listen to the *entire* thought of the other person rather than waiting impatiently for your chance to respond.

Next time you have a dialogue with your partner or a friend, observe yourself. Don't be eager to answer. It's not a competitive tennis game, and you don't have to hit the ball back to win a point. Slow down your responses; become a better listener. As you do that, you will notice less pressure within you and more clarity of mind. You will understand clearly what the other is saying, and when your turn comes, your reply will be effective. Patient listening enhances the quality of your communication. Your partner or friend will enjoy talking to you, knowing that you're truly listening to what is being said.

If a relationship is to be one of shared intimacy, it requires a level of sensitivity between partners that goes much deeper than conventional social relationships. Simply, you cannot talk over your partner and expect a loving response. Life might have mistreated you; your current neurotic defenses could be a result of an emotionally deprived childhood. Become aware of past influences that could be destructive in the present, and don't dump your frustrations and hostile feelings on your partner each time you have a dialogue. Your partner might be sympathetic for a while but cannot possibly be responsible for your unfortunate past. A normal partner wants to be with you, wants to love you, and expects to have your love. To convey your feelings, you need to consider what the emotional reaction of your partner might be. This is our challenge if we wish to have a loving interaction.

Good communication implies a basic understanding that at times we are as vulnerable as children. The complaining one may be the hurting child and the supportive one may be the compassionate parent. We need to remember that the one who takes on the parental role should do it with care and sensitivity and not keep the other in the state of a child. A balance is important so that one does not feel inferior to the other. Together with tender loving care, balance in communications as partners interact is of utmost importance. Simply, one cannot control or dominate the other, either through eloquence or assumed superiority.

As you enter the area of loving communications, keep in mind the four basic styles that couples use to communicate.

~ *Style I consists of passing on information.* "It's a nice day." "It might rain tomorrow." "I saw your cousin at the grocery store," and so forth. Usually very little emotion is involved. In our everyday conversations, we use this style to be sociable or friendly. It goes on all the time when people live together and know each other well.

~ *Style II tends to be serious.* One tries to manipulate the other, to impose upon the other his or her personal opinion. In marriage, it is used to blame, to demand, to control, to put down. This style can be used in subtle ways — for example, in persuading and advising — which are only thinly veiled forms of manipulation. Often it is used in the form of sarcasm, interpreted as humor. Invariably, this style carries a sting, and the recipient gets hurt.

~ *Style III is speculative,* looking objectively at what is going on, seeking explanations and possible solutions. It may not accomplish a lot, but it can lead to decisions about what needs to be done.

   When couples have a disagreement that results in a verbal fight, they use Style II; they blame and attack each other. This gets them nowhere, but maturity surfaces when the emotions subside and they move into Style III. The usual prelude is: "Let's be reasonable. We're behaving like kids. Let's act like adults and try to figure out what's going on."

~ *Style IV is a much desired style,* taking us into a new dimension — that of the shared life in which our individual joy comes through shared happiness in which we make ourselves vulnerable in order to achieve intimacy with another person whom we love and trust. In this style, you share with your partner whatever feelings you have, honestly and openly. You say, "Here's what I'm feeling right now. This is where I am." This sort of surrender needs to be made without blaming or attacking your partner and without defending yourself. This may not be a natural thing to do, but it brings results.

Identifying these four styles of communication can help restore a dysfunctional relationship or improve the conditions of a functional one, and make a good relationship better. Style II is not productive; be careful it does not sting your partner. Styles III and IV will give you and your partner a new life and greater hope for happiness.

Suppose you have made up your mind to work on your relationship. How effectively you convey that commitment is a major issue. How you talk to each other and how you respond to each other's emerging needs is crucial. Initially, you may feel hesitant or even reluctant to make the first attempt. You may be afraid that your effort will fail or that you will say something that will make matters worse. Deep down, you may not be confident that your partner will be receptive. If feelings of this kind are bothering you, they should be faced. If you have a commitment to give your relationship a chance, in all sincerity pull back and take time out to consider your new approach. If communication has suffered all along in your relationship, restoring it will have some consequences. It will take sensitivity and patience to speak to your partner with love, especially if he or she is resistant. Both of you may need to sit down and explore your feelings. It may be that neither of you has the motivation to work on your relationship. If that is so, you may be missing all the good things that could come out of growth in your relationship. If you doubt your ability to communicate, you might seek a competent counselor to help you get started. Are you willing to accept this sort of direction?

Sometimes one person is more eager than the other to repair the relationship. This is not uncommon. The hesitant or unwilling partner may be just as honest as the willing partner in wanting to restore the relationship. What she or he needs is an act of special love and loyalty. Ideally, a relationship begins to blossom and bear fruit when both are ready and eager to begin to talk the language of love.

Communication is one of the most powerful factors influencing the quality of any relationship. Couples often share many years together — the same interests, same house, same bedroom — but some partners feel like roommates; there is no soul-to-soul contact. Initially they want to share and be intimate, but as time passes, they find themselves drifting apart. They communicate ideas and facts, they talk about other things and other people, but rarely share their personal feelings about each other. Of course, in sharing personal feelings there is a risk. The one who listens may disapprove or even reject what is being said. Any time we express a deep personal feeling, we become vulnerable: "Now my partner will know the truth about me, and I can't stand that, because I don't like the truth about me."

When and how do we learn to communicate? As soon as we are born. As infants, we begin to communicate with our surroundings. By the age of five, we have had a million experiences. We have developed ideas about our image, how others see us, what we can expect, and what is possible or impossible. In early childhood, we figure out, often by trial and error, what we have to do to get what we want. The communication that worked for you as a child was basically compatible with your family's style of communication. As you matured and gained insight, you added your own rules or beliefs to help you cope with life. The communication patterns you developed earlier in your home of origin may continue to affect your present life.

We know that living with another person requires a much more sensitive system of communication than we ever learned at home or in the wider circle of society. In our ordinary daily contacts with other people we are continually practicing deception or withholding the truth. When a friend in the street asks how you are, you automatically say, "Fine, thank you." If you were to tell the truth — that you have a headache, or that you had an angry argument with your daughter — your friend would hardly know how to respond! Usually you do not tell people about personal things like that; it is just not done. When your neighbor shows you a new dress that she bought, you say something positive, even if you really think it is ugly. Holding back your real thoughts or feelings — and even the true facts — is simply part of the accepted social code of behavior. It can be justified; our relationships with these people are not intimate and personal. Only a small part of their lives touches an equally small part of our lives, so there is no need to disclose to them personal information of our more private selves.

However, marriage is an entirely different kind of relationship. It brings two people together in the closest possible intimacy to share each other's lives and to try to meet each other's interpersonal needs. In that kind of relationship, an altogether different system of communication is required. In our social relationships many of us have little chance to learn the more intimate kind of communication. Our current culture, with all its advancement and sophistication, fails to provide an educational system that prepares us for an intimate relationship like that of marriage. How, then, are we to learn?

If you are uncomfortable with the way you and your partner communicate, answer honestly the following questions:

1. What kind of communication did you observe between your father and mother? How did you feel hearing adults talking in your family?

2. Were your parents cooperative and trusting, or competitive and challenging? Did you witness quarrels that made you feel uncomfortable?

3. Was one parent always right and the other always wrong?

4. Was one parent dominant and the other a submissive?

5. Were both passively cooperative or actively aggressive?

6. If you grew up with one parent only, how did you communicate with him or her?

7. If you were raised by surrogate parents, what kind of messages did you receive from them?

We are all, to a great extent, influenced by parental patterns. Some of these may be beneficial to our adult life while others may be destructive. In whichever way we are influenced, it is important that, as we interact in our relationships, we observe what is good and works with our partner. Whatever seems hazardous must be left behind.

You are aware how uncomfortable it feels to be misunderstood by your partner or how uncomfortable it is to have the desire to share something and yet have difficulty in finding the right words. Communication is an art. It requires an awareness of the other person's being; it requires a thorough awareness of who you really are. To that knowledge, add acceptance, flexibility, effort, patience, and skill. The reward is good, for healthy communication brings us closer to our partner. The word "communicate" literally means "to become one with."

It has been said by specialists that the average couple spends between twenty-two and twenty-four minutes per week communicating with each other, and that includes time spent on trivial questions such as, "Where is the *TV Guide?*" or "What time will dinner be ready?" or "Would you mind taking out the garbage?" Truly, this is a sad commentary on people who love each other and have such an emotional investment in each other.

Of course, you may decide to defy statistics and make communication a primary goal in your relationship. Start with the daily dialogue. Appropriate fifteen minutes each day when you and your partner will talk. Find a comfortable spot in your home, sit and look at each other, and begin a conversation. Here is a simple exercise:

Think of yourself as a video camera equipped with sound. You are face to face with your partner. Your senses take in what your partner looks like and sounds like, and your brain reports to you what this experience means to you. Perhaps your partner reminds you of someone else in your life. Meanwhile, your partner is going through the same experience. You have no way of knowing how your partner feels within unless you are told. By the same token, your partner has no idea how you feel within yourself. It is important to your partner to know how you feel within yourself, if he or she wants to communicate with you. It is important for you to know how your partner feels within, if you want to communicate with him or her. It is dangerous to assume you know how the other feels. It is better to ask. Do not assume that your partner knows how you feel. It is better to tell how you feel.

Our personal perceptions and our beliefs influence communication with our partner. When we are positive about ourselves and about life, interaction becomes interesting and brings satisfaction. When we operate in a negative framework and we are pessimistic about life and living, we bring discouragement to our communication with our partner.

Nobody enjoys listening to a negative person who cries the blues and cannot see anything good in life. Negative beliefs can be a major source of irritation, bringing discord to a relationship. Your belief systems influence what you say about yourself, your feelings, your actions, and communication. This is truly a sensitive area. Through the practice of self-acceptance and self-improvement, you can turn to your partner with a positive smile of affirmation. As you encourage yourselves regularly, you can replace negative beliefs with positive attitudes, such as:

~ I want to love you and to make you happy.

~ I want to understand you, but I need your help.

~ I want to cooperate when we deal with important issues.

~ I feel good about our relationship.

~ I feel equally responsible for our life together.

~ I like to be fair to people. I want to be fair to you.

~ People treat me fairly. I want you to treat me fairly.

When you hold to positive attitudes, you will notice a strength in your feelings. The strength of each feeling will make conversation a pleasant experience. Feelings are not by themselves good or bad, but they can be used in a positive or negative way. They are reliable sources of information and can be used as tools in strengthening your relationship.

As you communicate with your partner, you need to listen not only to what is being said (the message) but also to the feeling. Missing or failing to recognize the feeling in a message may result in the misunderstanding of the entire message. You may deduce, for example, that your partner is mildly disturbed or annoyed when, in fact, the feeling is anger or deep hurt. Until we understand the underlying feeling, known as metacommunication, we cannot effectively understand the message. By communicating your feelings to your partner and by listening for the feeling in your partner's voice, you allow growth in your relationship.

Like children, relationships grow daily. You and your partner become more mature and face life's adventures with an understanding that promotes good feelings. Since no partnership or marriage is perfect, yours or mine included, it is important to realize that certain attitudes and beliefs can prevent a relationship from improving. Attitudes such as those reflected in the following statements may cause conflict. They may block communication; at worst, they may break up the relationship.

~ "I'm a man." Meaning: Don't ask me to do a woman's job.

~ "I'm a woman." Meaning: I can't do a man's job.

~ "I know I'm right." Meaning: I don't need to hear what you have to say.

~ "I'm just that way. You know how I am." Meaning: Don't expect me to change.

~ "It's your problem." Meaning: Don't expect me to bail you out.

~ "Take care of it yourself. They are your relatives." Meaning: I don't want to get involved.

~ "If you had only listened to me in the first place, this would never have happened." Meaning: I'm always right. I expect you to listen.

~ "You should anticipate my desires and feelings." Meaning: By now you should know me.

~ "Why do we have to discuss it?" Meaning: I've made up my mind.

~ "Can't you guess what I'm feeling?" Meaning: You ought to be able to read my mind.

~ "If we really love each other, why do we have to talk about this?" Meaning: Love conquers all.

These statements are roadblocks preventing healthy communication, our own maturation, and happiness. We have an opportunity to choose another approach which invites our partner to participate effectively in our life.

Share, Understand, Negotiate

One of the neglected areas of communication between partners, and the most important for a loving relationship, is disclosure of positive feelings. When partners have been deeply moved by something or touched by a tender observation that strikes a note of response in them, they should try to express it, to disclose it to the other, and capture the moment before it is gone. With positive self-disclosures, that is, by telling of the good things you feel, partners can open up the way for honesty in more critical areas of feelings and knowledge of each other.

"Okay," you say, "but what can I do with my negative feelings? If I reveal how I truly feel — frustrated, disappointed, angry — I may hurt my partner's feelings. It's better to keep my mouth shut."

As wise as silence seems to be, it is intangible. It is hard to get a handle on, and it's impossible to respond to a silent person. Not giving the other a chance to respond is a form of punishment. It becomes a barrier to communication.

The concern you might have — protecting your partner from your true feelings — is probably the concern you have about yourself. You are afraid you will feel less good or weaker than your partner expects you to be, or that your partner will not approve of your feelings. What is really in operation here is a lack of personal identity and the sense of insecurity that goes with it. That insecurity leads us to maintain the facade, to appear as the ideal partner, and, thus, to live a superficial life. But are we ideal? We are only human. To hide what we really feel makes it difficult to mature and achieve the knowledge of each other that is possible only through caring communication.

Great progress can be made when both partners are willing to cooperate in improving their methods of communication. If one partner is resistant, the task is more difficult. However, since you are responsible only for your own behavior, it is not your job to change your partner. As you change, manifesting a positive approach, you will influence your partner. If you are more empathic and understanding and if you avoid judgment, blame, and criticism, your partner may choose to see the positive side of you and respond to you with greater understanding and love.

When you communicate on a level, equal plane, you demonstrate that you accept responsibility for your behavior and are sensitive to your partner's feelings. "Any significant relationship starts with me" is an excellent guide for communicating effectively. Think of the acronym SUN–Share, Understand, Negotiate — and become the sun in your relationship for an entire week. You will notice a brightness, a warmth, a great feeling for each other. Practice your SUN.

Sharing:
> Instead of focusing on who is right and who is wrong, consider sharing your ideas and feelings without fear of rejection. Share, but don't intimidate the other. Examples:

> > ~ "I felt angry when you invited your mother over without telling me. I have no problem when your mother visits with us, but I would like to know ahead of time."

~ "I felt uncomfortable when you were late and didn't call to let me know. Now, I'm really happy that you're here. I would appreciate a call when you're going to be late."

Understanding:

It is difficult to understand the other unless you ask questions and clarify for each other what is said or felt. As you seek to understand your partner's thoughts and feelings, you demonstrate caring, respect, and love. Examples:

~ "Tell me how you feel when you want to go out on Friday evening and I want to stay at home and relax."

~ "I get the impression that you are anxious each time you go for a job interview. It must be difficult."

~ "I think that your idea of a vacation is visiting your parents. I prefer to visit them for a few days and then move on. I would like to see some other parts of the country."

Negotiating:

In respecting the individuality of the other, you treat each other as equals. You consider each other's ideas with respect and try to develop alternatives based on those ideas. The more the alternatives are developed together, the easier it is to reach a satisfactory agreement. Examples:

~ "Having a full-time job and then coming home to do all the domestic chores is overwhelming to me. I need your cooperation. What kind of chores do you prefer?"

~ "You sound very tired."

~ "I feel that I have no personal time at all."

~ "I was not aware that you needed some time for yourself."

~ "I would like to have Saturday morning for myself."

~ "I'll do the vacuuming and the laundry. Is there something else that needs to be done?"

Communicating, understanding, supporting, and empathizing encourage your partner to pursue personal needs. As a result of such personal fulfillment, the person comes back stronger, more loving, and more cooperative. The relationship, then, is not a burden but a process of facing life's difficulties with courage and joyful anticipation.

Keeping the lines of communication open means making time each day to catch up on each other's thoughts and feelings — and regarding this as a priority. It means learning to be honest about your own shortcomings in thought, word, and deed. It means accepting negative feelings from your partner without hitting back, because you realize that negative feelings shared with you will hurt you much less than if they were concealed and allowed to fester.

The Bible tells us to "speak the truth in love." There is no more important art than this to be understood and practiced by couples. It is the open secret of the successful relationship.

For Your Consideration

You should consider answering the following questions together:

- ~ How can you and your partner develop a more intimate relationship? Agree as to what could be your first step.
- ~ What factors influence the way you and your partner communicate? Make a list of these factors and discuss them carefully, one at the time.
- ~ How do perceptions about yourself influence your communication? Explore the accuracy of your perceptions?
- ~ What important information do your feelings give you?
- ~ How can listening and giving feedback help you identify your goals in a relationship?
- ~ What are the roadblocks in your life with your partner?
- ~ What areas of your communication need to be improved?
- ~ Dialogue is to your relationship what blood is to your body. When the flow of blood stops, the body dies. When dialogue stops, your relationship withers and resentment is born. Avoid resentment; introduce a loving spirit. For two weeks decide the night before what time you are going to have your daily dialogue on the following day.

FIVE

LOVE AND
LIVE LONGER

The beginning of love is listening attentively,
accepting the uniqueness of the other
while respecting each other's privacy.

∽◇◇∾

Can you be emotionally present in another person's life
without high expectations?

Chapter 14

WHAT IS LOVE?

Love is the essential substance of life:
We either love or perish — and without love,
we begin to perish at this very moment,
since without love there is no life,
but only the beginning of death.

— JOSE DE VINCK

Love concerns the heart. "Heart," here, means not the physical organ that pumps blood through the body, but rather the center of human emotions, desires, and affections. With the mind, we become informed; with the heart we become involved — and love means getting involved.

Love cannot be easily defined, for if you have never experienced love, no one can describe it to you. Dictionary definitions are inadequate. Statements of sages and wise teachers about love may inspire us for the moment, but gradually we have to arrive at our own inference, according to our needs and perceptions.

When we raise the question, "What is love?" it's like asking a corollary question, "What is God?" We find ourselves in a sort of mysterious quandary about how to answer. If we have grown up in a loving environment where we felt accepted, loved, and secure, we might be able to give an answer. If, however, we were brought up in a hostile, nonsupportive, or even abusive environment, lacking basic care and security, then it would be difficult to describe love with a sense of confidence.

You must have heard countless definitions of love. Writers and poets praise love in prose and song, and by now you may have come up with some definition of your own. It's good if you have had even a tinge of loving experience and feel something about it.

It's a starting point, which may help you to revise or even improve your perception of love.

In my early adolescent years I believed I was in love and was convinced this was ideal love. Later on in life, I experienced romantic love, that forceful emotion that precipitated my marriage. There was no greater love than ours, my wife and I thought. Later, as we matured, we discovered that love was beyond fantasies and poetic lyrics. Love meant action, care, concern, and consideration for the other's being. Growing up without a mother, I admit that even during my mature years, I had a problem dealing with the true essence of love. I wrestled with the question: What does it mean to love? I read, spoke, and wrote about it. Eventually I became aware of another love, a powerful love — my wife nursing our infant. This most natural state of love, Pat mothering Katina, our baby, had such an impact on me that it never left me.

In awe, I observed my wife unconditionally giving of herself to our child, day and night at different hours, according to our infant daughter's need. She had no training for this activity, but she knew in her heart what was required. Pat gave Katina not only flesh, blood, and bones; she also held her on her breast, admiring, singing, and talking to her. She nursed her for several months, giving part of her body and spirit that our child might grow up healthy and strong. She knew what to do and when to do it, and she did it without any expectations. Yes, there were tough times and many inconveniences, but Pat was willing to take the worst that our child had to give and respond only with love and affection. It is evident that motherly love portrays the best model of how to fully love.

Without this love that mothers feel for their offspring, we would have perished not too long after birth.

Examples of human love are abundant; people express or repress them according to their emerging needs and perceptions. While motherly love is evident and highly praised, there are mothers who cannot give sufficient love. Many people, having been wounded in childhood or not being loved in adulthood, can only go through the motions of loving when they become parents. Yet, love expressed out of obligation lacks dignity.

Motherly love cannot be only a mother's prerogative. Some mothers can love more than others, and there are mothers who feel obligated to show their love. Single or married women who are not mothers are also capable of loving. Women and men who love a person, a priceless possession, a truth, an ideal, a faith are willing and ready to dedicate their lives to it. Countless women and men dedicate themselves to caring for an ailing parent or child. Others invest years in scientific research and in the healing arts. Many people eager to do charitable work become missionaries in poverty-afflicted countries and with sacrificial love help to elevate the condition of the less fortunate. Most of these efforts reveal the deep yearning of the human heart to love and to heal.

Love is a powerful force; it is an amazing energy-like electricity that can supply light for an entire city once the switch is turned on. It is a multifaceted emotion that can perform miracles in human life. When you decide to love, you bring fulfillment and happiness into another person's life and you create a healthy environment for growth. Love is a decision. We are born to be loving. You want to be loving. I want to be loving, but each person needs to learn about love by experience. Love implies action. If you don't know how to swim, reading a description about swimming will be of no benefit. Simply, you need to get into the water and learn the basic strokes and eventually the skills of swimming.

Surely most of us can define sex. Sex is an act between two people. Sexuality is a natural part of a loving relationship between a man and a woman. If you put two normal people who are attracted to each other in a room by themselves, they will have no trouble figuring out how to express attraction and fulfill themselves through sex. Sensual attraction and sexual fulfillment play important roles in enhancing marital love. However, we are all aware that the sexual act is a confined experience and it is ephemeral. As powerful and pleasurable as it can be, it has a beginning and an end. It is contained, and it has boundaries.

On the other side of the coin, love is complex and must be learned. Love is an inner process that we bring to a relationship. There are no strings attached to the loving. No returns are expected, only an interest in the other person's wellness. The common expressions "I love you and you should also love me," and "I do this and that for you, so you must do something for me," do not help a relationship last. What lasts is a love that is spontaneous and comes from within. Once it starts, it must be maintained and reinforced constantly, otherwise it fades and dies. To be told about love is like telling a child who has never tasted candy about fudge. A taste can do what words cannot. Once you have an authentic human relationship, you'll know it is like no other experience you have ever had in your life. Yes, you can learn to love by loving.

The experience of love is a choice we make, a mental decision to see love as the only real purpose and value in any relationship. Love in your mind produces love in your life. A great beginning to loving a person is friendship. The Greeks call it *philia,* which means feeling good and relaxed in the presence of another person, feeling accepted, not judged or criticized, simply wanting to be with that person. Creating a climate of relaxation is not only comforting and reassuring, it also nurtures growth. *Philia* requires that we accept the person with whom we like to be, in his or her totality, and we provide for that person what we would like to experience ourselves.

Romantic love tends to be blind and often irrational; friendship, however, is rational and based upon respect rather than passion. Without liking and respecting the other, genuine love cannot be achieved. Mutual respect is essential and it helps to establish one's identity and equality, as well as healthy communication between partners. Starting with respect and appreciation for your partner's presence in your life, you are laying the foundation for love.

Love is based upon the identity and equality of both partners; it is generous and nonpossessive. As you begin to feel fulfilled as a person, love becomes the overflow of your own fulfillment. If you feel joyful within yourself, you want to see your partner just as joyful. To really love someone is to have a feeling of belonging with, rather than to, another person. To genuinely love another, you must wish or even enable that person to attain a state of contentment.

Love: Agape and Eros

The ancient Greeks recognized and had words for two kinds of love: *agape* and *eros.*

Agape is unconditional love, nonpossessive, and demands nothing. It is a strong wish to see the other person grow according to his or her own potential and be happy. It does not criticize, evaluate, judge, or discriminate. It arises out of a feeling of self-sufficiency, wholeness, confidence, and strength, not out of feelings of need, greed, or emptiness. A true image of agape is the mother nursing her child, not when the infant is crying because it is hungry, but when she feels the milk overflowing from her breast.

Think of a farmer who, although advanced in age, continues to plant trees. He does not expect to sit under their shade or eat their fruit, which he may never see. He prunes and nurtures them out of the fullness of his heart, gratitude, and the joy he experiences in life itself. It is the effort that counts, not the results. Agape-love is regarded as the attitude and nature of God, who "sends rain on the just and the unjust equally."

Eros is possessive. A person in a state of eros is enslaved by the object loved — for example, a man who claims to be madly in love with a woman. Is he really? Or does he desire to possess her being? He controls her thoughts, her wishes, her behavior in an effort to keep her. Is that love or bondage? Fueled by racing hormones, eros deals with preferences, ego-trips, physical desires, and acquisition. Anyone accustomed to the tensions, anxieties, hostilities, and uncertainties of the struggle to possess and dominate, even to exploit, the other would have difficulty in understanding what agape — true love — is.

The qualities of agape-love are eloquently described in the Bible:

> Love is patient; love is kind; love is not envious or boastful or arrogant or rude. It does not insist on its own way; it is not irritable or resentful; it does not rejoice in wrongdoing, but rejoices in the truth. It bears all things, believes all things, hopes all things, endures all things. Love never fails.

Having some idea of what the difference between agape and eros is, you will understand why two people, who were so delighted at the discovery of each other and at the thought of the wonderful thing that had happened to them, wind up spending the rest of their lives wishing it had never happened. They may feel disappointed at making a bad choice, or blame their partner, or think that some other partner might make them happier. How is it possible that love, the most important building block of human society, ends up in a turbulent relationship or a hostile separation or divorce? Is there anything that we can learn from the ever-increasing number of breakups to gain some insight that might help us live a harmonious life?

Lynn, a very attractive professional woman, fell in love with Frank, a successful architect in Manhattan. On sight, we would probably consider them the perfect couple. She talked constantly about him. He was the best thing that had ever happened to her. Frank was everything she wanted in a man, and they decided to get married. After their glorious honeymoon on the French Riviera and toward the end of their first year of marriage, things had changed dramatically. The marriage fell apart; the couple separated, and Lynn lived with a girlfriend for a while. Frank stayed at the condominium they had bought together. Lynn was very angry with him. In her words, "He ruined my life. He is the worst thing that ever happened to me. He's an ambitious workaholic, a selfish male who is in love with himself and has no time for me. I hate him." She went on and on accusing him and blaming him for her unhappiness. Eventually, they agreed to divorce. "What happened to your love?" We might ask Lynn, "Why are you so angry?"

To appreciate the emotional impact of such an experience, visualize yourself in either Lynn's or Frank's position. As long as you were attracted to the other person and the other person fulfilled your needs and expectations, you accepted that person totally. That person and no one else was the ideal for you. Maybe you called that romantic acceptance the fulfillment of love. At some point in your relationship, one or both of you could no longer find joy and fulfillment, which started the chain reaction that led to lost interest in each other. Not feeling loved or being able to love the other resulted in anger, withdrawal, and frustration, which led to separation.

Was it genuine love? More often than not, sensual attraction, nature's cunning way of insuring procreation, is mistakenly equated with genuine love. If their relationship had been primarily true love, and not only secondary sensual love, then Frank and Lynn would probably not have ended in a divorce. If there had been at least a fair component of genuine love, once their initial needs were fulfilled, they would have proceeded to meet the next set of marital needs — respect, responsibility, and sincere interest in the happiness and well-being of each other — with reasonable effort and eagerness for the growth of their relationship.

A powerful relationship can develop when two people commit themselves to unconditional love, and to encouragement and support of each other's growth. Both must give freely, without selfish motives or the desire to lock the relationship into any preconceived mode. There are no boundaries when we fully embrace each other toward the fulfillment of our potential.

For Your Consideration

~ If you are feeling angry, betrayed, or hurt, can you at least take a little time out to rest your body? Let your mind slowly relax. Sit in a quiet, comfortable place and let your emotions settle. Let these turbulent feelings surface and dissipate like bubbles in boiling water. Soon you will notice that your sadness has evaporated and is replaced by pleasant feelings. You may even smile. Your smile is the sunrise of love. Cherish it as long as possible.

~ Love is a process that starts with a smile and anchors at the heart, not the physical organ, but the center of your emotions. Once it starts it has a purpose: to culminate in joyful relationship with a significant other. Are you willing to start this process?

~ A love relationship takes time, effort, and generosity. Can you truly say, "I give you all I have and all I am without expecting anything in return"? If anything does come back, what a gift!

~ How may times have you heard of someone who suffers from a broken heart? That person, once happy and in love, is in pain. Is it really genuine love that broke that person's heart, or was it sensuality and selfishness? True love doesn't break hearts. It only heals them.

~ Genuine love can bring you great joy. In stressful times, it can bring you relief. Think of the potential of being truly interested in the happiness of another person. Don't ever underestimate your loving ability, activate it. Try to show unconditional love to your partner for at least one week, and you will be pleasantly surprised at the results.

Chapter 15

CAN YOU LOVE?

Love involves much careful and active listening. It never promises instant gratification, only ultimate fulfillment.
— Barb Upham

Can you love? How you answer the question depends upon your perceptions of what love is. It is your personal choice to say, "Yes, I can love" and truly mean it, or "I cannot." Unless you have been emotionally damaged in early life, your ability to love is inherent; lack of it can hardly be understood in a human being. Beyond any doubt, you are able to love. Think for a moment of the loving feelings that you might have had for a very special person in your life. How happy you were at that time, knowing that your love was bringing happiness to another person. You were in love with life itself — every part of it, good and bad, painful and pleasant. This is the attitude that you need to nurture. If you were able to love then, it is likely that you are capable of loving again now. You have nothing to lose but plenty to gain. Give yourself a new chance.

Visualize yourself at the end of a long, particularly difficult day. How good it is to be able to return to a partner or a friend, to someone to whom your feelings matter. Like a child, you can come for parenting, and like a mother or a father, the other can take you in. It's the sort of momentary comfort that sets the stage for a pleasant evening, but what proves most important is that this brief and loving contact gets both partners through a lifetime.

Being available and willing to listen to the other with sympathetic caring and understanding needs to be reciprocal. The "parenting" partner must not presume to take over or to tell the "child" what to do about the day's hurts. Rather than actually trying to take care of the other, that night's parent need only be personally available to sense the feelings expressed in the other's complaints and create a soothing climate. What truly needs to be communicated is: "I'm here for you, and I care. I'm sorry you're having such a hard time. I'm willing to listen to your hurt because you hurt, and to be respectfully careful not to tell you how you should feel or what you should do."

If this can be done without forgetting that you are both adults, then tonight's "parent" can be tomorrow night's "child." This is a prime ingredient for a loving relationship.

Theodore's Secret of Success

Love, as a creative energy, sustains and propagates life. It cannot be forced on anyone — that is, you cannot be forced to love a certain person, and you cannot force anyone into loving you. Sincere love comes from the heart, not as the result of obligation, guilt, or other external pressure, but as an unconditional gift to a significant other.

Theodore saved his marriage by unconditional love. He was a middle-aged high school principal, with an interest in physical fitness. His wife, Lisa, a twenty-nine-year-old mother of two boys, was an up-and-coming assistant in a prestigious financial firm. Handling home, family, and job became a burden. At work, a drink with lunch became a daily routine to help her relax. Spent and exhausted, she returned home in the evening to face another stressful situation — children who needed their mother's attention, and a husband who claimed that she didn't have to work. They could live on a smaller income, he insisted. Lisa's struggle between the corporate world and her family life caused a major conflict. While seeking a sensible solution, she began to drink heavily. Her husband and children felt neglected, and the marriage began to go downhill with increasing speed. Although they both went to marriage therapists and explored several marriage counseling modalities, Theodore decided that what his wife really needed was total and unconditional love. I was not exactly sure what he meant by unconditional love. He explained that he was surrendering to the process of loving, not asking questions, not judging, not wanting to change her, but making every possible effort to observe and fulfill his wife's wishes.

It's good that Theodore was able to surrender to the process of loving, and it worked for him. Other people feel hurt; their emotions are damaged; they feel angry with their partners. How can they give them unconditional love when they are haunted by bad memories? They cannot forgive. Do they have a choice? They do. If they truly wish to restore their relationship, they can. It's not easy, but it can be done. Don't ever doubt the potential and the ability to love. People were created to love, and the capacity to love is inherent. The choice is to explore it.

For a precious moment, go back to the time when it was exciting to be with the person you chose as your partner. Beyond the sexual attraction that you felt, you found a person who not only accepted you the way you were but also accepted what you were trying to be or do. It felt good to be with that person who, unlike most of the other people in your life, did not judge you or want you to change. The world took on a rosy hue. With this person, you could relax, go to places, laugh at everything and have fun. It was rewarding to learn about that person who seemed to care for you without reservations. The more you learned about that person, the better it felt, and of course you reciprocated generously. You had found someone with whom you could share your world with no fear of rejection, ridicule, criticism, blame, or complaint. This willingness to share your dreams, hopes, and fears is known as love; it became your relationship. The ability to love is within you, and it develops gradually. Can you revitalize that ability and give your partner unconditional love?

An important aspect of love is that it is blind. When a person is "in love" or perhaps "infatuated," there is a marked over-evaluation of the loved person and an underestimation or a denial of the deficiencies. The loved person is seen by the lover as perfect, ideal, or even divine. In Theodore's marriage, the lover turned out not to have been blind but to have been perceptive of potentialities in his wife that outsiders could not see. His searchlight of love discovered and developed the love relationship in their marriage.

"That's good for Theodore," you might say, "but I don't think it could work for me." You may be right. Many partners doubt their potential or may not be as perceptive and willing as Theodore. So, let's move on with our searchlight and define love according to your potential.

Love, a Many-Splendored Thing

Many of us who did not receive sufficient nurturing love in early childhood may have a hard time loving another person. We want to be loved by someone, but it is difficult for us to return love. Simply, we didn't learn how to love, although the potential for loving was there, a God-given quality inherent in every human being. As adults we can activate this personal potential for a good purpose. It is a choice.

Love is such a many-splendored thing and subject to so many differing definitions that it is easier to start with what it is not: that is, pseudo-love.

The "love-sick" spouse talks about love and gives love as though it were a thing to dump on another person and that the other person would then appreciate. The "love-sick" partners give themselves as objects to be made happy by the "fortunate" receiver of their gift. Since this type of love tends to be felt as a burden by the other person and engenders resentment, it might be called pathological love. Its goal is to be in fusion with the other. As in an infant-mother relationship, the infant is a burden and is loved for itself, not for what it gives or does. In marked contrast, mature love is a state of being in which the satisfaction or security of another becomes as important as one's own.

Mature love recognizes the strivings of the other person towards dependency and independency and preserves each partner's integrity as an individual self. It implies a relationship of mutual trust and respect, and it allows for the expression of the maximum potentialities of each person for giving and taking. In this state of love there is caring, respect, concern, consideration, compassion, and affection for the other person and not simply mutual exploitation or mutual satisfaction of needs. As in a satisfactory sexual encounter, one does not give and the other get; both give and receive at the same time. This is not an idealized description of love; it is a promising prescription of the possibilities that you and your partner can share.

Love, like money, is meant to be given to another for a good purpose. There is a major difference between money and love, however. If you keep giving your money away, eventually you will have none. The opposite is true about love. The more love you give away the better you feel and the richer you become. Being able to say the words "I love you" is the first step. To go beyond the first step, you need to realize that love is an inner process that you bring to your relationship. If you have read the book thus far, you are serious about applying love as the most powerful medicine for healing. This sort of love needs to be unconditional. Giving love with no expectations is the secret of your success. Initially, there is very little else that you need to know. Practice this love with your partner, without conditions, and you will find yourself feeling an inner joy that you probably never felt before.

"What if my partner," you might say, "doesn't respond or even rejects my unconditional love?" It is unlikely, but if it happens, don't lose heart. You have no control over the other person, but you have to go on with your loving feelings. You have made a commitment. Suspend any negative thoughts about your partner's reaction and wait. The love that you make available to your partner has enormous power to heal and repair. It cannot happen instantly; it will take some time. Just maintain love in your heart, continue your loving approach, and let everything take care of itself.

This type of love is a force within you that will enable you to reconnect with your partner and provide a newness of life. It is the motivating power that enables you to give strength and power and freedom and peace to another person. It is not a result; it is a cause. It is not a product; it produces. Like electricity, it is valueless unless you use it wisely and for a purpose.

For Your Consideration

~ Suspend any blame that you have attributed to your spouse. Never point the finger at the other and say, "It's all your fault." It doesn't really matter whose fault it is; it matters that there is a rift in the relationship that needs healing.

~ Acknowledge honestly all aspects of your contribution to the breakup of your marriage and ask yourself, "What can I do about it? Can I accept some responsibility? Can I ask for forgiveness? Can I forgive?"

~ Examine yourself genuinely and decide what you are willing to contribute to make your relationship joyful and productive. Can you participate a bit more in your partner's life and show interest?

~ Ask yourself honestly how much actual sharing you are willing to do to meet the needs of the other. How generous and cooperative can you be?

~ As you minimize the existing stressors in your relationship, approach your partner with unconditional love. If love is energy, how constructively can you use it?

Chapter 16

ARE YOU LOVABLE?

There is only one corner of the universe you can be certain of improving and that's your own self.
— ALDOUS HUXLEY

You can choose to have a loving personality that will make you feel happy, beginning today. Love is a basic human need. We all want to be loved by someone significant in our life. In order to receive love, one must be lovable. Are you lovable? Reply, "I am lovable!" Repeat this over and over to yourself until it is firmly planted in your mind. Be thankful to yourself. Being able to love is about getting to know another component of your inner strength. This very moment you'll begin to sense that you no longer need to expect others to love you. A good start is to love yourself. This is not an egotistic notion. Wise teachers can share all that they know and yet maintain their knowledge, but first they must have the knowledge. Lovable persons share love and yet they still have love within. Loving yourself involves the discovery of the true wonder of you, not only the present you, but the many possibilities of you. Because you are lovable, your partner will respond to your loving self.

You have already put aside your need to be loved by a new awareness, your capacity to love. Now you can love with no expectations. This kind of unselfish love is encapsulated in J. Krishnamurti's words: "To love is the most important thing in life. But what do we mean by love? When you love someone because that person loves you in return, surely that is not love. To love is to have that extraordinary feeling of affection without asking anything in return."

What happiness it is to love and to be lovable!

The brutal frankness of Charlie Brown is hilarious because it is so true to life: "I love all mankind — it's people I can't stand."

We can redefine the practice of love by being loving. Remember that love is not finding the right person to love or be loved by. It is *being* the right person *of* love. Like the sun behind the clouds, there is always love behind your present condition — if we are willing to turn it on by being loving.

In *The Brothers Karamazov,* Dostoevsky writes: "Love all of God's creation, the whole and every grain of sand in it. Love every leaf, every ray of God's light. Love the animals, love the plants, love everything. If you love everything, you will perceive the divine mystery of things. Once you perceive it, you will begin to comprehend it better every day. You will come at last to love the whole world with an all-embracing love."

With Charlie Brown, you will declare, "I love all mankind." But unlike him, you will add, "And I love all people as I love myself." I am loving to my partner, even if my partner treats me unfairly. I love my partner, not because my partner deserves my love, but because I do — for life is for loving.

At this point of your reading, your resistances may rise. The negative things said about you may surface. You may start doubting your deeper loving qualities and believing whatever others think or say of you. Be careful. Put aside what others have said about you, ignore the definitions of your personality given by your parents, peers, teachers, and others who know you. Simply focus on the concept that you are lovable and capable of loving. Start believing it seriously. You are in charge of your thoughts; you have the ability to change any undesirable part of yourself and become a lovable person. Your thoughts about yourself are most important because they formulate your feelings. So let's briefly clarify what you might be thinking, saying, and feeling about yourself:

1. "I wish I could change my thoughts and feelings but I can't. That's the way I am. I have been this way since I was a child."

If you're truly comfortable with the way you are, there is no need to change. However, if certain parts of your personality are undesirable, then a change is called for. If you have a bad temper, if you are shy or fearful, if you feel angry or negative about your life, a change is possible. Stop believing that your personality is a piece of granite, hard and inflexible. You have the inner power to make new choices that will result in a different attitude. You can be gentle, more assertive, more patient, more positive, more loving and lovable.

2. "I wish I could change, but I can't. My make-up and chemistry are such that I can't help but be who I am."

Body chemistry, whether in your brain or in your stomach, may cause physical or emotional disorders that medical science can treat. It is important to trace the source of the problem. What's really bothering you that causes sleepless nights or excessive anxiety or bad habits? What prevents you from being loving and lovable?

3. "I wish I could change, but I can't. I'm just like my mother [or father, grandfather, uncle, and so forth]. My brother and sister are just like me."

Perhaps you are able to identify some of your characteristics that are similar to those of your father or mother. You can hold on to these as a defense against any favorable changes that you could make to improve your situation. We all share some similarities with our family of origin, but is this an excuse to maintain an unproductive or even destructive attitude? At which point can you take personal initiative and responsibility to change what is changeable? Can you honestly negate your part in life and feel that you are a victim of circumstances? Right now, whatever qualities appear to be objectionable, get rid of them. You may have a hard time eliminating certain influences that you experienced as you were growing up. At least be aware of them, reduce them, and don't let them persist in controlling your life. You are in charge of your life.

The above three barriers and whatever other obstacles you may be facing are leading us to a significant point. If you let go of any external, negative conditions and influences of your past, you can focus on the present. The force, vitality, and spontaneity that flow within you and keep your heart ticking can reactivate your emotion of love. You are capable of loving. You can be lovable. It is a skill and can be developed. You can re-create your self-image and restore a positive sense of who you are and what you can be. Consider the following three steps:

1. Create in your mind a clean and straight path, a lovable image that gives you both peace and joy. Rather than imitating others, as admirable as they may be, concentrate on an image that seems comfortably pleasant to you. More gentle and loving? Less irritable and happier? Less shy and more assertive? Less critical and more compassionate? Less judgmental and more forgiving? All these qualities are possible when you decide to eliminate negative thoughts from your mind and begin to trust in your ability to love.

2. Screen your emotions as they surface. They originate with your thoughts. Good thoughts generate good emotions. Bad thoughts generate negative emotions, and negative emotional reactions affect your attitude. Emotional reactions also affect your body. If you are upset, you get a headache. Some physical pains tell us that there is something wrong with us emotionally. We may get the latest medication for our physical symptoms, go on vacation, and sense temporary relief, but if we don't come to grips with what is really bothering us, we will never realize our potential for healthy living.

3. Love involves the willingness to face the inevitable pain and doubt, inevitable misunderstanding and dark moments. Whatever negative character traits you have developed over the years — depression, doubt, fear, unhappiness, pessimism — are habits of the mind that can change, once you make up your mind to be a loving and lovable individual. If you are willing, you have the power to change those things that do not work for you. If you believe this and know it within yourself, you will notice that you feel emotionally and physically healthier. You have all that it takes to make yourself a healthier and happier person.

Love — It's a Challenge

Think of yourself as an inexhaustible fountain of love. Visualize your partner coming to drink from this personal source. You will find yourself always available, a more generous giver and a more grateful receiver. Your partner will find you lovable, and you will cherish the experience.

What does lovable look like? It is not a state of perfection. Lovable people still have a physical presence to contend with. They can be as unkind and insensitive as anybody else, but when they realize their mistakes, they are quick to apologize. Reconciliation is a high priority for them. People who have tapped their love potential do not have a difficult time admitting they are wrong. Their internal love security system allows them the freedom to admit their faults and be transparent.

When circumstances wreak havoc with lovable people — a big fight, lack of trust, a major conflict — there will be some downtime, but they don't stay down. They refocus their attention on the big picture, acknowledge the truth that love is patient and endures all things, and move on. They don't allow disappointment and sorrow to control them. They don't deny or run away from their problems. They reset their minds on the power of love.

When lovable people are treated unjustly, they get angry, they feel outrage and frustration. There may be times in which thoughts of revenge cloud their thinking, but before long they regain perspective. They refocus on their loving self. They remind themselves of the time when they were able to love and the wonderful things that love accomplished. Do they feel the pain? Of course they do, but they look at their hurts differently. They choose not to become bitter. They forgive and move on.

The good things that happen once a person becomes lovable are all rational in nature. The presence of love makes a person more attractive and pleasant to be around. They are a joy to work with and for. Lovable people make for better customer relations, better marital relations, better parent-child relations, better friendships, better living.

It may be a challenge for you to be a lovable human being, but the effort is most rewarding, for it will build character that can endure any adversity in life. The challenge is promising:

~ To have love for those who do not love you in return.

~ To have inner joy in the midst of painful circumstances.

~ To have peace when something good you were expecting did not happen.

~ To have patience when things are not going fast enough for you.

~ To be kind toward those who are not very kind to you.

~ To be good toward those who have been insensitive to you.

~ To have faith when friends or relatives ignore you.

~ To be gentle when certain people treat you with arrogance.

~ To have self-control in the midst of intense temptation.

~ To have unconditional love for the person with whom you wish to live your life.

As I end this chapter, let me suggest an activity. Drink a glass of fruit juice and sit quietly in a comfortable chair. Take three deep breaths and relax. Then slowly and seriously consider the following:

1. You don't need to be right all the time. When there is a rift in your relationship, it is futile to question who is at fault. It is harmful to assume that you are totally right, and it's your partner's fault. It may make you feel superior, but a loving partnership is a relationship of equals. No one feels good when proven wrong. The one who is judged wrong will have a difficult time resuming a dialogue with you or restoring the damaged relationship. If you truly want your relationship to blossom and bear fruit, for one or two weeks simply let go of the desire to make your partner feel in the wrong and observe how differently things go for you. For starters, your self-esteem will rise. You will feel better and stronger because of your ability to love. You may even experience inner peace and joy. What about the other person who receives your love? He or she might question how genuine your love is and be skeptical of your intentions. Don't let that bother you. Eventually, when your partner recognizes your intentions, your love will help him or her to heal, to trust, even to love you again. Simply remain consistent and patient. Love requires persistence and endurance. Maintain your integrity as a person who can love.

2. You don't need to impose your good intentions upon your partner. Understandably, you would like to see immediate results of your unconditional love. Remember, the other needs to process your approach, your thoughts, your words, your actions. The loving thing to do is to allow your partner or friends the option of being themselves. If being themselves implies time away from you, your part is not simply to allow it, but to facilitate it lovingly. Kahlil Gibran's poetic statement, "Let there be spaces in your togetherness," is applicable here. Make every effort to help each other have that space. Treat that space as sacred. Taking time-out from each other to take a self-inventory, to heal, and to reevaluate your ability to love is the best thing you can do for yourself and for your relationship. Solitude can become your most meaningful companion, and it can assist you in being a more giving and loving person.

3. You don't need to possess the person you love. It is not fair to dictate how your partner should think, feel, or behave. Your partner is also an adult with an identity that took years to establish. You may want your partner to change. Change into whom? Perhaps, be like someone that you admire, or even be just like you? Is that fair to the other person? Remember the lyrics of the old song, "I love you just the way you are!" It is an empowering statement. What a joyful feeling to love someone unconditionally. When you are able to do this, you will experience a liberating feeling. In accepting the other without any expectations, you will feel both stronger and happier.

4. You don't need to understand everything. Upon waking up as each day begins, do you understand yourself totally? Not totally and not all the time. How, then, can you understand the thoughts and the behavior of your partner or of people around you? The ancient philosopher Socrates said, "One thing that I know is that I don't know." The fact that you are willing to say, "I do not understand, and it is fine," is the greatest understanding you can exhibit.

Since you have decided to explore the potential of unconditional love, relinquish your need to understand why your partner likes certain television programs, plays the piano at the same time everyday, goes to bed at a certain hour every night, reads certain magazines, and enjoys the company of colleagues at work. You are together not to understand each other totally, but to aid each other in living a life of love and purpose. When you give up the need to understand everything about your partner, you open up the gate to a garden of joy and delights. Then your partner has a choice to enter it or not.

EPILOGUE

As I bring this book to a close, I'm mindful of many troubled marriages that were on the brink of divorce. In exploring different options, the partners patiently and persistently tried to apply, one by one, the principles delineated in the five directives of this book. They found them supportive, and today many of the couples are cherishing a healthier and more productive life. Are their marriages now divorce-proof, free of conflicts? Of course not. No relationship is. In every relationship, as in every garden, a tiny snake periodically appears. It must be removed before it grows large and bites someone. Before a small disagreement becomes a major conflict, it needs to be resolved.

Are there no happy relationships? Does a marriage ever succeed — or fail? Or is it people who succeed or fail in giving themselves wholly to each other? Is it true that personally fulfilled individuals make happy partners? There are wholesome people who invest a very special spark and spirit, lending an aura of enchantment to their interaction with their mates. This may well be the secret of success.

However, there is the inescapable fact of divorce. Why do divorces occur? Is divorce wrong? Should people stay together "till death do us part"? Actually the percentages of divorces do not really tell the full story of the breakdown — for millions of marriages remain intact institutionally where they are totally divided emotionally. Is divorce immoral or is it more immoral to continue in a marriage that is emotionally and spiritually dead?

Divorce seems to be a solution for some people, inevitable for others, but it is costly emotionally, socially, financially, and physically. Children of divorced parents suffer tragic consequences that surface later in their lives. Divorce surely ends a marriage, but it does not end a relationship. The cloud of sadness of a lost love hovers over the survivors for a long time, if not for the rest of their lives. Partners struggle in their minds, seeking resolutions that, in many cases, are not easily attainable. Both spouses may argue that the divorce was not really their fault. Does it matter whose fault it was? Does it matter that once upon a time they loved each other very much? Perhaps not. Yet, as they hear the word "divorce," it matters.

In more than forty years, I have seen in my practice hundreds of turbulent marriages, dysfunctional families, disturbed individuals. Seeing those tearful eyes and agonizing faces, I feel their pain, I hear the cry for love, I sense their search for healing. Besides, I have traveled that thorny road myself. I went through a divorce; I know the pain. Today, as a licensed marriage and family therapist, empowered by professional training and years of experience, I present to my clients options for new directions, opportunities for healing and healthier living.

Every human being and every relationship goes through one or another crisis. We make mistakes, we hurt, we suffer, but we learn something. We learn that we are humans, and out of the chaos of life we manage to repair, to restore, to heal, and eventually to bring some joy and harmony into our fragmented lives.

For you to have read this book, there must have been a need. You have probably read other self-help books or heard wise words from other professionals. The final reality is that if there is a change to occur in your life, it has to begin with you. You can no more delegate others to solve your personal problems than you can appoint a surrogate breather. It is your life. Only you can be accountable for it. Only you can give it a new and more productive direction.

ADDITIONAL READING

Cloud, Henry, and John Townsend. *Boundaries in Marriage.*
Grand Rapids, Mich.: Zondervan Publishing House, 1999.
This book holds the key to mutual respect and provides tools
for making healthy and lasting relationships.

Leman, Kevin. *Keeping Your Family Together When the World
Is Falling Apart.* Colorado Springs, Colo.: Focus on the Family Publishing, 1992. This is a practical tool which presents
methods that can preserve marriages and raise children with a
minimum of hassle and heartache.

Nouwen, Henri J. M. *Here and Now.* New York: Crossroad, 1995.
This is an inspirational book. In a personal and insightful way
the author writes about the joys and sorrows, gains and losses,
hardship and rewards of human interaction and family life.

Smalley, Gary. *Making Love Last Forever.* Dallas: Word, 1996.
This book gets right to the root of the human condition and
offers real and invaluable advice on how to change the quality
of relationships.

Viscott, David, M.D. *How to Live with Another Person.* New
York: Pocket Books, 1974. This is a guide which points out
the little things that can either pull two people apart or draw
them together.

Wicks, Robert J. *Sharing Wisdom.* New York: Crossroad, 2000.
This is a pithy handbook which deals humanly with all manner
of people. In a commonsense approach, Professor Wicks shows
the benefits of reaching out and connecting with other persons.